Reflections of Southern Jewry

Reflections of Southern Jewry

•••

The Letters of Charles Wessolowsky, 1878-1879

edited by

Louis Schmier

Mercer University Press

This one is for you, Dad.

All books published by Mercer University Press are produced
on acid-free paper which exceeds the minimum standards set by the
National Historical Publications and Records Commission.

Library of Congress Cataloging in Publication Data

Wessolowsky, Charles, 1839-1904.
  Reflections of southern Jewry.

  Includes letters to Rabbi Edward B. M. Browne.
  Includes bibliographical references and index.
  1. Jews—Southern States—Addresses, essays, lectures. 2. Wessolowsky,
Charles, 1839-1904—Addresses, essays, lectures. 3. Jews—Georgia—Albany—
Biography—Addresses, essays, lectures. 4. Albany (Ga.)—Biography—
Addresses, essays, lectures. 5. Southern States—Ethnic relations—Addresses,
essays, lectures. I. Schmier, Louis, 1940-   II. Browne, Edward B. M. III.
Title.
F220.J5W47   1981   975'.004924   81-16995
ISBN 0-86554-020-9   AACR2

Table of Contents

• Acknowledgments •

No book prints itself, and though the author gets the credit line on the bibliographical citation, no publication can be produced without the invaluable help, guidance, and support of many people.

I will always remember the support and enthusiasm of Dr. Samuel Proctor, Distinguished Service Professor of History and Social Science at the University of Florida. Not only did he refuse to let me falter in this project, but the insights he added upon reading the letters helped immeasurably. I must also thank Arnold Shankman at Winthrop College in Rock Hill, South Carolina, and Abraham Peck, Assistant Director of the American Jewish Archives, for their comments regarding the historical value of Charles Wessolowsky's letters to the historiography of the Southern Jewish experience.

For the many courtesies and assistance in researching the life of Charles Wessolowsky, I will always be grateful to the staff of the Georgia State Archives, Anthony Dees and his staff at the Georgia Historical Society in Savannah, Gayle Peters and his staff at the Regional Federal Record Center at East Point, Georgia, the staff of Baker Library at Harvard University, Bernard Wax and his staff at the American Jewish Historical Society at Waltham,

Massachusetts, and to Jacob Marcus, Abraham Peck and Fannie Zelcher of the American Jewish Archives in Cincinnati. Special thanks must be given to Mrs. Sadie Gortatowsky Davis of Albany, Georgia, for consenting to an interview despite ill health.

In another vein, I would like to thank and acknowledge the support of Dr. Gordon Teffeteller, erstwhile head of the Department of History at Valdosta State College for allowing me flexibility in my teaching schedule to afford me maximum time to research this manuscript. I would also like to express my appreciation to the members of the Valdosta State College Faculty Research Committee, the Board of Directors of the Southern Jewish Historical Society, the Board of Trustees of the Valdosta State College Alumni Association, the trustees of the Harry Edison Foundation, and the Directors of the American Jewish Archives whose financial support made this book possible.

On both an endearing and technical note, I must offer a warm thank you to Mrs. Sarah Harrison, secretary of the Department of History at Valdosta State College, for bearing with me, enduring my sometimes unreasonable demands, and somehow interpreting a handwriting that more often than I want to admit bordered on Egyptian hieroglyph. She knows how much I appreciate her indispensable aid.

Finally, saving the best for last, there is little that can be put into words that would describe what I feel for the support and comfort freely and selflessly given by my lovely wife, Susie. For her toleration of my moods, for uplifting my spirits, for putting my frustrations into proper perspective, for snapping back when I snapped, for keeping me in my proper place, for her understanding, for sincerely sharing the exhiliration of my discoveries, for that I can only say a very intimate and cryptic "Just a little bit."

Louis Schmier
Valdosta, Georgia
July 1981

• Part One •

The Life of Charles Wessolowsky

The mood was somber as the Jews of the Thirty-second Regiment Georgia Volunteers gathered outside Savannah, Georgia, at Battery Harris on 6 September 1862. They were meeting that Tuesday morning to register their public protest against the expulsion of their fellow Jews from Thomas County in South Georgia two weeks earlier.[1] The noise of their individual heated debates and discussions stilled as Lieutenant Morris Dawson called the meeting to order. One of the organizers of the meeting, Charles Wessolowsky, came forward to speak. This twenty-three-year-old private from Company E was respected throughout the regiment as one of the ablest and best educated men within the ranks. Though noted for his outgoing personality and his ever-present wit, there was not to be any humor in his words or smile on his face this day. His language and gestures were sobered by a quiet anger at what he characterized as an "unjust act" taken against those of his faith who had been "falsely accused of profiteering." He lashed out against the citizens of Thomasville who he declared were trying to "clear their own skirts by asserting their nativity," and who were using the few

---

[1]The resolutions of expulsion were printed in the Thomasville *Weekly Times*. No copies of this issue survive. The resolutions were reprinted, however, in the September 10th issue of the Macon *Journal & Messenger* and again in the September 12th issue of the Savannah *Daily Morning News*. For background on this incident see Richard McMurry, "Rebels, Extortioners, and Counterfeiters: A Note on Confederate Judeaphobia," *Atlanta Historical Journal* 22 (Fall 1978): 45-52; Louis Schmier, "Notes and Documents on the 1862 Expulsion of Jews from Thomasville, Ga.," *American Jewish Archives* 32 (April 1980): 9-22.

Jewish residents and roaming Jewish peddlers as scapegoats to hide from anyone seeing "if they themselves don't partake of this extortion." With an unashamed pride in his heritage, Wessolowsky forcibly proclaimed that "as a people, willing as we were, and are, to struggle for our adopted country, to sacrifice all that is dear to us, to abandon our second home, and leave our wives and children to the care of strangers not belonging to our society, or fraternity, we, our armour buckled, enduring all toils and hardships of a camp life, ready to shed our blood for the defence of our country, now to be denounced, slandered, and accused of infidelity, and disloyalty to our country and government." He then challenged "the gentlemen of Thomasville" to "see how many Jews and foreigners, more or less, are in each [Georgia regiment]; ask them to peruse the lists of donations, and see how liberal and free-hearted the German Jews and foreigners are in behalf of aiding their adopted country."[2]

His listeners were mesmerized by the force of his words. Morris Gortatowsky sat awed, thinking for a moment that he had just "heard Moses thundering down from the heights of Sinai with admonishments to the Gentiles."[3] Under the same spell, the Jews quickly passed a resolution that Wessolowsky had helped draw up that denounced the "foul slander" of the Thomasville Resolution as "unbecoming and unworthy of Gentlemen" and that called for a boycott of Thomas County by all Jews.[4]

Tears swelled the young Wessolowsky's eyes and a tightness in his chest shortened his breath as he watched the confident determination in the faces of his fearless compatriots who came forward to boldly sign their names to the resolution. Years later he would recall this moment as one of the highlights of his life, for it

---

[2]Savannah *Daily Republican,* 20 September 1862.

[3]Interview with Sadie Gortatowsky Davis of Albany, Georgia, 25 August 1979. All references to this extensive interview are hereafter cited as Davis, 25 August 1979.

[4]Savannah *Daily Republican,* 20 September 1862. Many of the Jews who were involved in this and similar protests refused to let their memories fade, preferring to settle in towns such as Valdosta, Bainbridge, and Albany rather than in Thomasville. For background on this matter, see Louis Schmier, "The Man From Gehaus," *Atlanta Historical Journal* 23 (Fall 1979): 91-107; Louis Schmier, "The First Jews of Valdosta," *Georgia Historical Quarterly* 62 (Spring 1978): 32-50.

gave him an unshakeable confidence that America was truly the bastion of religious liberty in which bigotry and persecution had no place as they had in the Old World. The experience confirmed for him the fact that the Jews in America could combat hatred whenever and wherever it reared its ugly head.[5]

Paradoxically, it had not been a quest for religious freedom that had prompted Charles's parents to send their nineteen year old son to America in 1858. Their decision that Charles had to leave Prussia's Posen Province was influenced by a fear that if he stayed he might not escape from the dreaded military service in the Prussian army.[6] Indeed, their fear only heightened the anxiety that had been created by the revocation of the rights granted them as Jews by the Prussian monarch during the tumultuous days of the Revolution of 1848. With disillusionment and resignation replacing their earlier optimistic expectation, and with their economic situation worsening, the future for their children did not seem at all promising.

Charles's parents had come to these conclusions two years earlier when Charles's older brother, Asa, had approached

---

[5]Davis, 25 August 1979.

[6]Charles Wessolowsky was born in the village of Gollub, in the Prussian province of Posen, on 3 September 1839. The reasons for his departure were not unique to his or his brother's situation. Indeed, escape from military service in the Prussian army (serving a monarch who was obviously no longer sympathetic to the plight of the Jews living within his domain) was one of the chief reasons for the immigration of adolescent German Jews. Consequently, their departure was without fanfare. It was not an embarkation on a voyage for fame and fortune in a New World paradise; it was more of a sad and reluctant escape from immediate dangers that were so threatening that the Jews were willing to tear their families apart. This mournful exodus was prompted by a realization that all that remained in the ancestral villages were the warmth of selected memories, the cold fears of the present, and the fatalistic expectations for the future. That sullen sense of hopelessness created a state of depression that no amount of false or self-induced optimism generated by rumors of opportunity in the strange and unknown America could truly overcome. "America" was not a place for these Jews such as Charles Wessolowsky. It was a word elevated to an ideal out of desperation to get away from the pungent odor of terror that had made it difficult for them to breathe. For background on this immigrant experience, see Oscar Handlin, *Children of the Uprooted* (New York: G. Braziller, 1966).

conscription age. Their solution was to send Asa to a relative who had immigrated earlier to the United States, and who had settled down in a "strange sounding" place called Georgia. Since Asa's departure, the Wessolowsky family had been receiving letters from Asa in which he never stopped lauding his newly adopted country as a land of opportunity and freedom. Though faced with a similar dilemma, Charles's parents were not as quick to dispatch their second son as they had been their first. They hesitated to send Charles off to follow his brother's path because news had reached the family that Asa had become somewhat lax in the ritual observance of Judaism. Their hesitation proved to be only momentary, for America was Charles's only ray of hope as it had been for Asa. So, with a little traveling money in his pocket, a few pieces of clothing in a roped bundle, and a parental benediction in his heart, Charles left his ancestral village of Gollub. During the lonely hours at sea he kept thinking of both his parents' warnings about the lurking influence of "godless America" and of their urging that he never forsake the faith of his forefathers—that while he should learn to act as an American and speak as an American, he should never stop thinking as a Jew.[7]

Immediately upon landing in New York, the young Charles headed south. His money took him by railroad as far as Richmond, Virginia. From Richmond, he walked to Sandersville, the county seat of Washington County in northeast Georgia. If Charles was expecting to be greeted with excitement and open arms by his brother, he was mistaken. His brother was annoyed with the young boy for arriving one week later than expected, and he informed Charles that a valuable week's worth of peddling had been lost while Asa had waited for Charles to arrive. Years later Charles recalled that Asa seemed to be in such a hurry to "get on the road" that as he took Charles's travel bundle with one hand, he gave him a peddler's backpack with the other. "Uncle Charles used to chuckle," Sadie Gortatowsky Davis remembered with a smile, "that when he came to Sandersville his brother grasped his shoulders only to spin him

---

[7]Davis, 25 August 1979.

around to push him out the door through which he had just entered."[8]

Charles, however, refused to start peddling about the countryside the day after he had just finished a four hundred mile trek. Not only was he exhausted, but, as he scolded his older brother, it was the Sabbath. Actually, his call upon religious devotion was more of a tactic to delay venturing out into the countryside and to hide his fears of that journey. Sadie Davis remembers how Charles would laughingly remark how foolish he was in those days. But, to the newly arrived eighteen-year-old Charles, his fears were very real as were the potential dangers. Only when his brother virtually shoved him out of his house did Charles reluctantly accept his brother's promises that he would be safe in the wilds of Georgia.

"Uncle Charles would always smile or laugh as he described himself and how he felt on that first peddling trip," warmly recalled Sadie Davis. "There'd he be with his 'store' hangin' between his shoulders—that's what he called his peddler's pack—loaded with threads, needles, buttons, piece goods and other things. The pack was so heavy, he would say he would walk bent-kneed and hunched over. He didn't know the language or how to count in American money. He didn't know where he was or where he was really going. All his brother did was to point him in a direction, give a shove and say 'Geh!' (Go). There he was, alone among the trees, the wildest animals he could imagine . . . and the Gentiles. He'd give the loudest laugh as he said he didn't know which to be the most frightened of— the bears his brother warned him about or the first farmer he'd meet."[9]

To Charles's surprise and relief, he met neither ferocious bears nor devouring Gentiles. Instead, he found that the rural farmers were of a different breed of Gentile from those of his family's bigoted neighbors in the old country. He would never have thought a Jew could experience the warmth and friendliness with which he was received in the homes of his Gentile customers. He was

---

[8]Davis, 30 May 1979.
[9]Davis, 25 August 1979.

"stunned and speechless" the first time one of his customers asked him to eat with his family and spend the night in his house.

"The first meal Uncle Charles ever had in one of those farm houses was a piece of bacon," smirked Mrs. Davis. "He like to have died. He ate it because he was afraid not to, but he said he stayed up the whole night asking forgiveness."[10]

Charles returned to Sandersville from that peddling trip somewhat dazed. Not only were the farmers congenial, but they were grateful and helpful as well. They did not take advantage of his ignorance of the language, and they did not cheat him. He had to admit his brother was right. All would indeed be safe if he avoided the bears. Charles would soon come to think, however, that his brother was wrong in abandoning all religious observances as a means of eliminating outward differences from the Gentiles and insuring safety among them. The reception Charles had received and the respect accorded him on later trips would lead him later to the firm conviction that he would not have to survive in America, or become integrated into it, at the sacrifice of his religious devotion and practice. He often illustrated his position by pointing out to his brother how the farmers respected his religious observance and the extent they went out of their way to provide him acceptable foods once they learned what he could eat. That "Jew-hating" Gentiles could be tolerant towards a "Christ-killing" Jew seemed to indicate to Charles that honesty and sincerity were not only extremely important in determining personal relationships between Jew and Gentile, but could overcome generations of culturally bred fear, suspicion, and hatred.[11] In the months and years to come, Charles would argue with his brother and friends that the choice offered the Jew in Gentile America was not one of complete assimilation or isolation. Rather, an accommodation could be reached whereby the Jew could become an American socially, politically, and nationally, while remaining a Jew religiously, morally, and ethically.

Within a few months after his arrival in Sandersville Charles decided he would follow his own advice and become a part of this

---

[10]Ibid.

[11]Ibid.

new society rather than remain apart from it. His brother's means were too negative for his outgoing personality. Safety in distance and conformity was not suitable to Charles's independent and self-confident outlook. Because he was educated, though his extensive training was solely religious and none of the four languages in which he was fluent included English, his training provided him a framework of discipline wherein he could learn both the language and the culture of the land in which he was living.

He found the farmers were more than happy to help him learn English. While the adults would teach him the individual words for the various commodities he was selling, the children would take out their primers and would help teach him how to read. "Uncle Charles used to say," remarked Sadie Davis, "that the children got a kick out of being a teacher rather than a student. They used to play 'school' with him and even scolded him if he didn't mind their orders."[12] It was not long before Charles was packing a primer of his own in his backpack. He struggled through the pages at every opportunity— while he was walking between farms (which caused many a bruise as he stumbled over unseen obstacles); while he was resting; just before he went to sleep; and right after he awoke. In fact, the primer became his second "prayer book," for whenever he read from his prayer book he also read for at least five minutes from his primer.[13] After the primer, he graduated to reading literary classics. He would

---

[12]Ibid.

[13]The spiritual communion with God through prayer had been an integral part of the Jewish religious experience from earliest times. In the Jewish religion, prayers may be offered individually or congregationally. In Biblical times they were usually individual since meetings of the community occurred only at times of sacrifice. Regular congregational services date back only to the period of the Babylonion Exile in the 6th century B.C.E. With the destruction of the temple in 70 C.E., prayers were standardized and assembled into prayer books called *siddur* (pronounced sid-der) which means "order" or "arrangement." The prayer book used by Charles Wessolowsky was based on the prayer book compiled in the 9th century by Amram ben Sheshna in Surah, Babylonia. It includes the three daily prayer services: *Shaharith* (pronounced sha-ha-reet) or morning service; *Minhah* (pronounced min-ha) or late afternoon service; and *Maarib* (pronounced mar-eev) or evening service. The traditional Jew, as was first Charles Wessolowsky, prays or *davens* (pronounced dah-ven) three times a day and always faces east towards the land of Israel. The most important daily prayers in the prayer book are: the *Shema*

read these works aloud "to the trees and animals" in an effort to eliminate his accent and speak like the natives.[14]

In early 1859, Asa accepted his brother as an equal "partner" in their newly formed "company" that they established a few miles east of Sandersville in Riddleville. The "company of two," as one observer described it, was little more than a crude device designed to secure additional credit from the Savannah merchant houses.[15] On one of these credit-seeking trips to Savannah, Asa arranged a marriage for Charles. After all of the terms of the marriage had been agreed upon, on 24 March 1859, Charles married Johanna Paiser.[16] Morris, the first of three children, was born a little more than nine months later in Riddleville on 1 January 1860.[17]

With the added responsibility of supporting a family, Charles convinced his brother that it was time to strike out for greener pastures. In early 1861, the Wessolowsky brothers closed their Riddleville business and headed for Savannah.[18] Whatever plans Charles might have had for the future, they were altered with the

---

(pronounced she-ma) which is the passage beginning "Hear O Israel . . ." (Deut. 6:4), and which proclaims the unity and sovereignty of God, and is recited each morning and evening; the *Amidah* (pronounced ah-mee-dah) which means "standing up" because the prayer is recited quietly while standing. The *Amidah* is the extraordinary prayer of *Shemonah Esreh* (pronounced shi-mo-nah ess-ray), which means Eighteen Benedictions, that is offered three times daily. It involves thoughts on wisdom, learning, and immortality. It extols God's glory; it offers a hope for the welfare of the one who prays, his family and community; and it thanks God for His blessing. Also repeated three times a day are the adoration prayers of Psalm 114 and the *Alenu* (pronounced all-ain-u). For a detailed discussion of Jewish religious services, see A.Z. Idelsohn, *Jewish Liturgy and Its Development* (New York: Henry Holt & Co., 1932).

[14]Davis, 25 August 1979.

[15]*Records of R.G. Dunn Co.*, Georgia, vol. 35, p. 175, Harvard School of Business, Baker Library, Manuscript Division, Cambridge, Mass. Hereafter cited as *Dunn*.

[16]Georgia, Chatham County, Probate Court, *Record of Marriage Licenses, 1851-1866*, p. 101.

[17]*Population Schedules of the Eighth Census of the United States, 1860*, National Archives Microcopy No. T-653, Washington County, Georgia.

[18]*Dunn*, vol. 35, p. 172. National Archives, Record Group 58, Department of the Treasury, Records of the Internal Revenue Service, *Internal Revenue*

bombardment of Fort Sumter. On 7 May 1862, Charles, who had been sent to this country to avoid military service, enlisted along with his brother as a private in Company G, Fifty-seventh Regiment, Georgia Volunteers. "Both he and my daddy," explained Sadie Davis, "believed they weren't going to do any fighting. But as my daddy said, 'Fifty dollars for a sign-up bounty looked mighty inviting and was a lot of money for doing nothing'."[19]

At first that judgment seemed accurate. The unit was reorganized as Company E, Thirty-second Regiment, Georgia Volunteers, and was assigned to the unassuming task of garrison defense of Savannah. It was during this period that Charles displayed both his command of his adopted language and his leadership ability when he led the protest against the expulsion of the Jews from Thomasville.

Immediately after the incident at Thomasville, however, the regiment's situation changed. The Thirty-second Georgia was moved north for garrison duty at Charleston, South Carolina. For the next two years, Charles fought in minor engagements as his unit was moved up and down the east coast protecting the Atlantic ports of Jacksonville, Savannah, and Charleston. As a consequence of his valor in combat, he was given a battlefield promotion to regimental sergeant major. It was another lesson for this young Jew about the rewards of becoming part of the hitherto alien Gentile world without having to renounce his heritage and faith. On 28 November 1864, his military career came to an end. His regiment had been moved from Charleston to Marietta, Georgia, as part of the force defending Atlanta. At a skirmish at New Hope Church in Dallas, Georgia, a few miles southwest of Marietta, Charles Wessolowsky was captured. He spent the rest of the war at Hilton Head prison.[20]

At the close of the war, he returned with his family to Sandersville. The destruction wrought by Sherman's troops to the

---

Assessment Lists, 1865-1866, Annual 1865, Division 8, District 3. Hereafter cited as *IRAL*.

[19]Davis, 25 August 1979.

[20]Charles Wessolowsky, *Compiled Service Records of Confederate Soldiers Who Served in Organizations from the State of Georgia*, National Archives Microcopy No. 266.

area and the lack of available goods, however, made it impossible to start a business.[21] By the beginning of 1866, he was back in Savannah operating a small general store with his brother at the corner of Broughton and Habersham Streets.[22] His knack for business, however, could never reach the heights of his skill with words. Despite a growing postwar boom, he was unable to stave off his creditors. Leaving his brother in Savannah, he traveled 120 miles west to Albany, Georgia, lured there by promises of success offered by his cousin, Adolphe Kieve, and an old comrade-in-arms, Morris Gortatowsky.[23]

Unfortunately, Wessolowsky did not leave behind in Savannah what was then judged "his poor practice for money."[24] He went into partnership, at the advice of his cousin, with one of the local Jewish merchants. And though the business thrived for about eighteen months, it eventually failed under circumstances "that smacked of fraud" as one observer noted.[25] For the next few years, he drove a wagon throughout the counties of southwest Georgia, peddling all kinds of dry goods. He next went into an unsuccessful business partnership with his cousin. "Uncle Charles used to tell us how the Gentile folk would joke with him," recalled Sadie Davis, "that he couldn't be one hundred percent Jewish since he didn't have any knack for business. 'You sure there ain't some of us in you?' they'd poke at him."[26]

Apparently his limited economic success and a general recognition that he was without any business sense had little effect on the extent of both the social and political position he was achieving in Albany. For though his friendliness and charm were likeable traits to both Jew and Gentile, it was his learning, his

---

[21] *Dunn*, vol. 35, p. 172.

[22] *Purse's Directory of the City of Savannah* (Savannah: Purse & Son, 1866), p. 142.

[23] Savannah *Daily News & Herald*, 7 July 1866; 28 August 1866; Davis, 25 August 1979; *IRAL*, Annual 1866, Division 5, District 1.

[24] *Dunn*, vol. 10, p. 290.

[25] *Dunn*, vol. 10, p. 291.

[26] Ibid.; Davis, 25 August 1979.

qualities as a leader, and his willingness to apply himself in community affairs that caused the citizens of Albany to ignore the defect in his commercial pursuits.

Almost from the moment of his arrival in Albany, the thirty Jewish families there agreed he should be their leader.[27] His extensive biblical and talmudic training, his fluency in Hebrew, his knowledge of ritual and ceremony and his oratorical ability were credentials they could not ignore.[28] For his part, Wessolowsky accepted this position within the Albany Jewish community

---

[27] *American Israelite,* 20 August 1869.

[28] The Talmud (pronounced Tol-mud) is a massive compendium of sixty-three books. Included in it are debates, dialogues, conclusions, commentaries, commentaries on commentaries, commentaries on commentaries on commentaries, of scholars and rabbis who for over 1,000 years applied their interpretation of the *Torah* (Five Books of Moses sometimes called the Pentateuch) to the issues of law, ethics, ceremony and tradition. It is not meant to be merely read, but to be studied! The first division of the Talmud is called the *Mishna* which means "repetition." It is a more advanced interpretation of the original expositions of the *Torah* called the *Midrash*, "exposition," begun by Ezra and Nehemiah. It is a collection of interpretations of biblical laws amassed between the 5th century B.C.E. and the 2nd century C.E. These laws were originally transmitted orally. Thus the *Mishna* is known as the "Oral Law" as opposed to the *Torah*, the "Written Law." The second division of the Talmud is the *Gemara* (pronounced ge-mar-ah) which means "supplement." It is a collection of commentaries on the *Mishna* written between the 2nd and 5th centuries C.E. The legal parts of the Talmud are the *Halakah* (pronounced Ha-la-ka), the "law." The ethics part of the Talmud is called the *Aggadah* (pronounced ah-gah-dah) which means "tale." The entire collection is the sum of rabbinical thought on every then-known subject. The Talmud, however, is not dogma or catechism. It is the explication that formed Judaism's common code of law, morals, ethics, and obligations. It was probably the greatest force in preserving the unity of the Jewish people in the Diaspora. As soon as the Jewish child had some grounding in the Bible, he "dove into the sea of the Talmud." Indeed, study in Jewish tradition of both the Scriptures and Talmud was considered greater than observance of ritual. The sages said that an ideal man is one who studies, is honest, and speaks gently to people. In fact it was believed that study led to observance. Consequently, Jewish boys would begin studying as early as the age of three and rarely remained illiterate past six. The Torah was the only elementary text followed by the Talmud. So important was education in Jewish tradition, it was said that the presence of a school was more important than a place of worship. For a further exposition on the Talmud and Jewish education, see Louis Finkelstein, ed., *The Jews,* 3 vols (New York: Schocken Books, 1973).

because, as he was to write later, "the golden calf alone does not constitute the happiness of man, and that religion in its pure and untarnished state, with its teaching of morality and truthfulness, is also essential and requisite for the unalloyed pleasure and felicity of this world."[29] For the next twenty-three years, until the Jewish community acquired the services of Rabbi Edmund Landau, Charles Wessolowsky performed all the services demanded of a religious leader.[30] He led the religious services both during the Sabbath and special holidays, performed the burial rites, presided over marriages, consecrated cemeteries and dedicated newly constructed temples.[31] At times, in conjunction with his peddling trips, he acted as a circuit rabbi performing similar services for Jews living along his route.[32]

In addition, as "patriarch" of the Albany Hebrew Congregation he felt obliged to insist that his fellow Jews perform their social duty

---

[29]See the letter from Charles Wessolowsky to Rabbi Edward Brown dated 13 October 1879, written from Jackson, Mississippi, p. 155.

[30]There is no leading central priestly authority in Judaism. The term "rabbi" means "my teacher." It is a title conferred upon a man learned in the Jewish religion. The title was first used in the first century at the time of the destruction of the Temple in 70 C.E. The rabbi is not a priest or minister; he is neither an intermediary between God and man, nor a spiritual arbiter. His traditional position gives him no power or hierarchical status within a Jewish community. The authority of the rabbi rests solely on his learning and personal character as well as the subsequent respect accorded him by the members of the community. The rabbinate was institutionalized only in modern times. Nevertheless, the rabbi still enjoys no priestly privileges. In orthodox Judaism he rarely leads the services, and only recently did the rabbi assume the duties of a Sabbath preacher offering sermons. The title "rabbi," then, was given to those men learned in Jewish law, making the distinction between a rabbi and a layman somewhat vague at times. Traditionally the rabbi is a teacher of Jewish lore and law. Today, the rabbi functions much as a clergyman of other religions functions. For additional information, see Finkelstein, *The Jews.*

[31]*The Jewish South,* 14 October 1877; Albany *Herald,* 8 July 1904; Albany, Ga., Albany Hebrew Congregation, *Book of Sermons by Laymen and Members, 1870-1895,* American Jewish Archives, Box No. X-127.

[32]Georgia, Lowndes County, Court of Ordinary, Marriage Book A., pp. 52, 257.

as prescribed by Jewish law.[33] Under his guidance, the congregation formed a Hebrew Benevolent Society for the purpose of distributing charity to the needy. Always looking to the future, Wessolowsky also organized a Sunday School in which he and his wife provided the religious and moral training of the congregation's children, which he felt was vital if Judaism was to survive in the United States.[34]

Wessolowsky's zeal was not confined solely to serving the religious and moral needs of Albany's Jewish community. Haunted by the ghosts of Thomasville and drawing upon his personal experiences, he felt that it was essential for the Jewish community to earn the respect of the Gentiles and to demonstrate to them that the Jews can contribute to the vitality and stability of the town. While a few of the Jews were active in civic affairs, none displayed the energy

---

[33]Charity is called *tsedaqah* (pronounced tse-dah-kah) which means "righteousness." There is no separate word for "charity" in Hebrew. "Charity" also infers the obligation to establish justice by being righteous, upright, compassionate and, above all, helping one's fellow man. The obligation to help the poor and needy is one of the cardinal religious duties of the Jew. Indeed, the Jewish religion never separates charity from the duty to act justly and generously. Charitable acts are, then, indispensable for a moral life. Such acts are more important than ritual observance, for they are signs of devotion and complements to prayer. One essential ingredient of being charitable was never to shame the recipient. Every Jewish community, therefore, placed great stress on helping the poor, the sick, the handicapped, and—in the United States—the immigrant. Every community had a special fund for the needy; every holiday included philanthropic activities. Every home contained a charity can of *pushka* (pronounced push-keh). The highest form of charity is to help someone help himself; next, was to help anonymously and secretly. Jews are flatly forbidden to ignore or turn away anyone who asks for help. In the United States, the Jewish community institutionalized or organized all charitable activities into "Aid Societies" or "Benevolent Societies." For further discussion, see Finkelstein, *The Jews*.

[34]*American Israelite*, 20 August 1869 and 21 October 1870; Davis, 25 August 1979. Eight years later Wessolowsky helped the women form a Hebrew Ladies Benevolent Society as the attention of the men was diverted to insure the contruction of the congregation's temple. See Albany, Ga., Albany Hebrew Congregation, *Hebrew Ladies Benevolent Society Minute Books, 1876-1957*, entries of 20 February 1878 and 17 February 1901, American Jewish Archives, Box No. X-166; Albany, Ga., Hebrew Ladies Benevolent Society, *The Golden Jubilee and Memorial Fund*, p. 153, American Jewish Archives, Box No. X-129.

and enthusiasm upon which Wessolowsky drew. "He sometimes felt as if he alone could bring Jew and Gentile together by presenting himself as a representative of all of what a Jewish citizen truly was. And he succeeded in showing that the Jews could help the town if given a chance and weren't regarded as just a bunch of 'outsiders'," explained Mrs. Davis.[35]

Consequently he always refused to be hindered by any possible negative reaction that might result from such attempts. Indeed, he was prone to lay the blame for such adverse reactions at the feet of the Jews. To his way of thinking, it was their responsibility to stand up and claim what was rightly theirs as guaranteed by law; it was their responsibility to demonstrate to the Gentile majority that they did not threaten the stability of society; it was their responsibility to earn the respect of the Gentiles; and it was their responsibility to educate the Gentiles and thereby eliminate the source of their ignorance in which were bred suspicion, fear and hatred.[36] "He once said, as I recollect," remembered Sadie Davis, "that sometimes he felt like a Jewish missionary among the Gentiles to show the way for other Jews to follow."[37]

The Gentile citizens of Albany began to feel the effects of his mission almost the moment he arrived in town. The point of his initial contact was Albany Masonic Lodge, Number Twenty-four, and later Albany Chapter, Number Fifteen of the Royal Arch Masons.[38] The members of these lodges, who included the most prominent citizens of the town, quickly came under the same spell that Charles cast over anyone with whom he came in contact. That spell would translate itself into a respect, admiration, and even a near reverence.

His road to prominence began in 1869 when Wessolowsky volunteered to be a floor manager of the Lodge's annual Calico

---

[35]Davis, 25 August 1979.

[36]Baton Rouge *Daily Advertiser*, 30 May 1878; Natchez *Daily Democrat & Courier*, 1 June 1878; *The Jewish South*, 7 June 1878.

[37]Davis, 25 August 1979.

[38]Letter of Carl F. Lester, Secretary of the Grand Lodge of Georgia to Dr. Fred Lamar Pearson of Valdosta State College, 3 February 1978.

Ball.[39] The efficiency with which he organized and managed the ball made it the most successful gala event ever held by the Lodge. Impressed with his leadership, personality and organizational abilities, the other members of the Lodge elected him to an office at the first opportunity. Indeed, some of the influential members of the Lodge felt that, regardless of his faith, he had something to offer the town.

At the end of 1869, Wessolowsky was persuaded to run for the office of alderman on the "working man's ticket of A.C. Westbrook."[40] Though he was not elected, the absence of any anti-Semitic response to his attempt gave him the impression that he should try again in the immediate future. In 1870, in spite of business difficulties, Wessolowsky ran successfully for alderman. His political career continued when, from 1871 to 1875, he held the position of clerk of the superior court of Dougherty County. His chief credential for this office was his flowing and legible handwriting. In 1875, he was elected to a two year term as state representative, which was followed by a one year term as state senator. He was the only Jew to have held all these elected offices.[41] There was even some discussion in political circles at the end of 1877 about nominating him for the United States Senate, but nothing came of it.[42] Nevertheless, Wessolowsky had opened the way in Albany for other Jews to follow. For the next fifty-five years, it was axiomatic that a leader of the Jewish community would sit on the board of aldermen and later on the city council.[43]

During the session of the state legislature in 1875, Wessolowsky attended a lecture given by Rabbi Edward B. Browne on the ethics of the Talmud.[44] The two men met after the presentation and

---

[39]Albany *News*, 21 December 1869.

[40]Ibid., 28 December 1869.

[41]*History and Reminiscences of Dougherty County, Georgia* (Albany, Ga.: n.p., 1924), pp. 82-95; *Manual and Biographical Register of the State of Georgia for 1871-1872* (Atlanta: Plantation Publishers, 1872), p. 114; Albany *Herald,* 8 July 1904.

[42]*The Jewish South,* 14 October 1877.

[43]*History and Reminiscences of Dougherty County, Georgia*, pp. 95-102.

[44]Edward Benjamin Morris Browne, nicknamed "Alphabet" because of his initials and academic credentials of an M.D. and LL.B., was born in Kaschau,

discussed the topic. Browne left Atlanta impressed not only that he had discovered a Jewish state representative who was "honoring Judaism," but one who was learned in Talmudic law. What seemed at the time to be little more than a passing conversation took on greater importance when, in 1877, Browne was elected rabbi of the Hebrew Benevolent Congregation in Atlanta.[45]

Immediately after assuming his position, Browne prepared for the publication of a weekly newspaper he called *The Jewish South*, and which was designed to be the region's first Jewish newspaper. Because of the demands of his pulpit responsibilities and a myriad of other activities in which he was involved, Browne was looking for an associate editor who could assume the duties of editing the newspaper whenever necessary. To his surprise, Wessolowsky's name was always mentioned by whomever Browne sought out for

---

Hungary in 1844. He came to the United Stater shortly after the Civil War when he served on the faculty of the Savannah Hebrew Collegiate Institute. He then went to Cincinnati where he put his university education he had received in Hungary to use. He studied for the rabbinate under Isaac Meyer Wise and earned an M.D. from the University of Cincinnati. In 1869, he went to Montgomery, Alabama, as that community's rabbi. One year later, he was elected rabbi of Milwaukee's Temple Emanu-El. During his tenure there, he earned an LL.B. from the University of Wisconsin. In 1871, he was appointed rabbi of the Jewish community in Evansville, Indiana and edited a newspaper entitled the *Jewish Independent*. From 1873 to 1876, he served the Peoria Jewish community while going on the lecture circuit; his topic was "The Talmud: Its Ethics and Literary Beauties." In 1875, he gave this lecture in Atlanta. Two years later, he was offered the pulpit of the Hebrew Benevolent Congregation in Atlanta which he served until 1881. During that three year period he edited *The Jewish South*, tried to establish a private boarding school which he called The Southern Educational Institute for Jewish Boys, and stayed on the lecture circuit. See Steven Hertzberg, *Strangers Within the Gate City: The Jews of Atlanta, 1845-1915* (Philadelphia: Jewish Publication Society of America, 1978), pp. 60-65.

[45]The incorporation of the Hebrew Benevolent Congregation in Atlanta was filed on 1 April 1867 by Samuel Weil. The Congregation assumed the Hebrew Benevolent Society formed in 1860 and the Union Sabbath School organized in 1847. Its first rabbi was D. Burgheim of Nashville. The congregation held weekly Sabbath services in rooms rented from the Masonic Lodge. The cornerstone for the congregation's temple was laid at the end of May, 1875. The building was dedicated on 31 August 1877. See Janice O. Rothschild, *As But a Day: The First Hundred Years, 1867-1967* (Atlanta: Hebrew Benevolent Congregation, 1967).

advice and help in his search for an assistant. Aside from general character references, Browne was particularly impressed when told that Wessolowsky would regularly endure the difficult trip from Atlanta back to Albany to perform his duties as patriarch of the Albany Hebrew Congregation.[46] Browne was equally impressed with Wessolowsky's growing involvement with B'nai B'rith.[47]

Wessolowsky's first experience with the fraternal order of B'nai B'rith occurred in Savannah where he joined Joseph Lodge Number Seventy-six in 1866 and rose to the position of vice-president.[48] At first, the lodge meant little more to him than a meeting place for Jews searching out the comfort of associating with their own kind. His attitude changed, however, after he joined the Masonic lodge in Albany. The sense of unity and camaraderie generated not only within the lodge but between lodges in different towns indicated to him that the B'nai B'rith order could serve a similar and sorely

---

[46] *The Jewish South*, 14 October 1877.

[47] B'nai B'rith means "Sons of the Covenant." The International Order of B'nai B'rith (I.O.B.B.) is the oldest and largest Jewish service organization. It was founded on 13 October 1843 by twelve Americanized German Jews in New York. Its first president was Isaac Dittenhofer. The establishment of an independent secular Jewish fraternal order outside the auspices of any synagogue and unrelated to existing models of communal organizations was an innovation which in some ways represented a radical break with the traditional practices. The new organization was consciously modeled after fraternal orders which these Jews had encountered in America, especially the Masonic Lodges and the Odd Fellows Lodges. Part of the incentive for the organization of B'nai B'rith seems to have come from difficulty experienced by some Jews in gaining admission to these lodges on account of their religion. B'nai B'rith was a secular organization with religious overtones. It was a membership organization reponsible only to its constituency, but it began to assume obligations involving the welfare of the broader Jewish community. The Hebrew Benevolent Societies were designed only to help the destitute; and the local synagogues were too preoccupied to provide mutual aid. As a result, the fraternal order, which cut across congregational lines, was able to concentrate on providing mutual aid and a sense of Jewish fellowship so desperately needed by the Jewish immigrants. The lodges maintained sick-benefit funds for its members as well as funds for widows and orphans. The payment of membership dues was a type of insurance policy. For additional information, see Leon A. Jick, *The Americanization of the Synagogue, 1820-1870* (Hanover,.N.H.: University Press of New England, 1976).

[48] Savannah *Daily News & Herald*, 7 July 1866.

needed function among the widely scattered Jews. Upon his arrival in Atlanta in 1875, Wessolowsky realized that the dispersal of the Jews throughout the land was not the only problem that threatened a sense of Jewish unity. For during this period, the Jews of America were experiencing religious division, as rituals and ceremonies underwent examination, and as traditional observances and practices were re-evaluated. The ensuing debates and opposing positions that are associated with the attempts of American Jews to decide whether to move from traditional Judaism to reform Judaism, and if so, to what extent, were already replacing Jewish unity with a disjointed mosaic.[49] B'nai B'rith, however, with its emphasis on advancing the rights of Jews and promoting both cultural and educational activities, could unify Jews around their traditional moral and ethical responsibilities without touching upon the sensitive and divisive religious issues in much the same way as the Masonic order was able to bring together men of different persuasions who otherwise would be mutually antagonistic. Wessolowsky later observed in a letter to Rabbi Browne:

> A wonderful band of Union that B'nai B'rith order! How it tends to make one feel, being a member of Israel's great family.
>
> In olden times, before the prayer book was multiplied, the Jew

---

[49]Early Reform Judaism is rooted in the period of political emancipation and cultural adaptation of European Jewry beginning in the 18th century. Israel Jacobson of Westphalia was among the first leaders to express the desire for modification in Jewish ritual. He introduced a number of changes into his synagogue: a mixed choir accompanied by organ music, a few prayers spoken in German, and a sermon presented in German. Samuel Holdheim and Abraham Geiger laid the ideological foundation for Reform Judaism. Geiger saw Judaism as an historical developing faith and rejected basic beliefs and practices which he believed were contrary to scientific thought. Holdheim agreed with Geiger about the need for reform, but felt that with the destruction of the Temple in 70 C.E. only the religious elements of Judaism—monotheism and morality— had validity. All ritual and ceremony connected with the Temple worship, however, had to be considered abolished. In America, Holdheim's views were better received than those of the more moderate Geiger. Indeed, Reform Judaism was divided for a time between a moderate and a radical movement. Among the leaders to found Reform Jewish institutions was Isaac Mayer Wise. He advocated the prophetic ideas of the Bible and declared the Talmudic regulations governing observance as no longer applicable. For the Messianic era he substituted a hope for a perfect world achieved

was at home whithersoever he came. No matter though a
stranger to all the world when he entered the House of God he
was *at home*. The modern tendency of American Judaism, has
alienated the Jew from his brother. Every place has another
prayer book; you enter a synagogue and you are a stranger.
What a sad transformation. Thanks to Providence B'B Lodge
is now the supplement, and no matter where you are, the same
work, the same sign, the same spirit, you are *at home* and
amongst brothers indeed.[50]

Browne was sympathetic to Wessolowsky's deep concern with
the need to reestablish a sense of brotherhood among Southern
Jews. Moreover, Wessolowsky's activities had some very practical
advantages for Browne's prospective weekly, for Wessolowsky was
about to be elected to the high position in B'nai B'rith of vice-
president of the Grand Lodge of District Number Five.[51] As vice-
president, Wessolowsky's renown and subsequent contacts
throughout the Fifth District of B'nai B'rith which included the
coastal southern states could prove useful to the promotion of *The
Jewish South*.

With all these factors in mind, Browne offered the position of
associate editor of *The Jewish South* to Wessolowsky. Even though
his term as state senator was about to end, Wessolowsky was
hesitant about accepting Browne's proposition. Browne was the
religious leader of the reform-leaning Hebrew Benevolent
Congregation in Atlanta. And though Wessolowsky was not close-
minded about the needs for possible change in the worship of
Judaism, he was not totally committed to the reform movement. He
advised Browne that he would not consider a position with *The
Jewish South* if the weekly was being designed as a periodical that
would preach Reform Judaism, Wessolowsky underlined his fear
by pointing out that since Browne was a protege of Isaac Meyer

---

by cultural and scientific progress with the mission of the Jews to spread godliness
in the world. See David Philipson, *The Reform Movement in Judaism* (New York:
MacMillan, 1931); W. G. Plaut, *Rise of Reform Judaism* (New York: World Union
For Progressive Judaism, 1963).

[50]See the letter from Charles Wessolowsky to Edward Browne from Mobile,
Ala., dated 3 March 1878.

[51]*The Jewish South*, 8 February 1878.

Wise, the founder of the American Reform Movement,[52] he wanted specific assurances that *The Jewish South* would not be a mere regional organ of Wise's newspaper, *The Israelite.*

Browne assured Wessolowsky that he would "stand fearless and independent" and would not champion one form of Judaism over another. Among the aims of the newspaper, Browne explained, involvement in the combative liturgical and theological arenas was not included. As Browne ran down the list of purposes he had set down for the newspaper, Wessolowsky perked up: the newspaper would be an educational instrument attempting to heighten the cultural awareness, as well as to increase the basic religious knowledge of its readers; it would be a clearinghouse for news about the activities of Jews and Jewish communities in the South; it would create a network of news of events of particular interest to Southern Jews; it would be a Southern-based and a Southern-oriented newspaper free of the "northern" perspectives and biases emanating from Cincinnati, Philadelphia, and New York; it would be an instrument of unity that would promote by whatever means

---

[52]Isaac Mayer Wise (1819-1900) was a pioneer of Reform Judaism in the United States. He was born in Steingrub, Bohemia. After studying in various Jewish academies (Yeshiva), he became the rabbinical officiant at Radnitz. Because of bleak prospects, he immigrated to New York in 1846 and became rabbi of Congregation Beth-El in Albany, N.Y. There he introduced reforms in the ritual and ceremony, such as choral singing, confirmation, and mixed pews, all of which were designed to improve public worship. In 1847, he conceived the idea of developing a single ritual for the diverse American Jewry and issued a call to establish a union of congregations. In 1850, he almost became the rabbi of congregation Beth-Elohim in Charleston. In 1854, he went to Cincinnati as rabbi of Congregation B'nai Jeshurun where he remained until his death in 1900. In that same year, he began publishing a weekly, *The Israelite*, later known as *The American Israelite*, and a German supplement *Die Deborah*. In 1856, he published *Minhag America* ("American Ritual") which modified traditional Jewish ritual and ceremony. He began advocating three goals: a union of congregations, a common prayer book, and a college to train American rabbis. The Union of Congregations was formed in 1873. Wise next concentrated on one of the Union's expressed aims—the establishment of a rabbinical college. In 1875, he became the first president of Hebrew Union College. By the time of his death, he had become one of the founding fathers of Reform Judaism. See James G. Heller, *Isaac M. Wise—His Life, Work and Thought* (New York: Union of American Hebrew Congregations, 1965).

possible a sense of common interest and that would create a common ground on which all Jews, regardless of their religious position, could stand together; it would be a promoter of a Jewish sense of brotherhood that would emphasize the activities of fraternal lodges such as B'nai B'rith; and finally, it would inform the Gentiles of Jewish ways and thereby would drain the swamp of ignorance in which breed the diseases of hatred and bigotry.[53]

With an unsure political future and little economic prospect in Albany, Wessolowsky accepted Browne's offer.[54] For the next four years, until his departure from the newspaper in August 1881, Wessolowsky served as associate editor of *The Jewish South* and promoted his three watchwords: pride, unity, and conciliation.[55]

It was during his tenure as associate editor that Wessolowsky wrote the letters to Brown collected in this volume. The occasions for dispatching these letters were two-fold promotion trips taken by Wessolowsky in mid-1878 and in the late summer of 1879. One purpose of Wessolowsky's travels was to promote *The Jewish South* and secure additional subscriptions for the newspaper. Another reason for Wessolowsky to "take to the road" was to go on the lecture circuit to spread the word about the importance of B'nai B'rith to the survival of American Judaism. His travels took him through more than sixty cities, towns, villages, hamlets, and crossroads in Alabama, Mississippi, Missouri, Arkansas, Louisiana, Tennessee, and Texas. So deep was his sense of pride in the fortitude displayed by his fellow Jews in their attempt to become a part of American society and still retain their Jewish identity, that he wanted to share his observations of the Jews living in these communities in the hope that such descriptions would encourage other Jews living in the South to persevere in their efforts to keep the "family of Israel" together.

On August 5, 1881, after *The Jewish South* had moved its offices to New Orleans and after Browne had left the newspaper,

---

[53] *The Jewish South*, 14 October 1877.

[54] Ibid.

[55] *The Jewish South* was first published in Atlanta. In late 1878, its offices were moved to New Orleans. With the exception of the 5 August 1881 issue which is located in the Manuscript Division at Tulane University, only issues dating from 14

Wessolowsky resigned his position by offering pressing business interests as the reason for his departure. Upon his return to Albany, however, Wessolowsky engaged in a series of mediocre business ventures until he went into partnership with his son Morris.[56] Never a merchant at heart, Wessolowsky directed his energies into other areas. He immediately reclaimed his position as patriarch of the Albany Hebrew Congregation. It was largely through his personal efforts that the congregation built its first synagogue in 1882 and its second in 1896. He served as a continuous member of the congregation's board of directors, and between 1889 and 1894 served as the congregation's president.[57] As he continued to promote an active religious life in the Jewish community, he also renewed his "mission to the Gentiles." Though he did not again enter the political arena, he devoted himself to serving the Masonic lodge. From 1895 to 1897, he held the lofty position of Grand High Priest of the Grand Chapter of Georgia, Royal Arch Masons; and from 1897 to 1898 he was Worshipful Master of Albany Masonic Lodge Number Twenty-four.[58]

Interspersed with the demands imposed on his time and energy by both his congregational and lodge activities, Wessolowsky lectured throughout the South promoting the causes of Masonry, B'nai B'rith, and Judaism. During one such lecture in Tampa, Florida, in March 1904, he suffered a stroke. Four months later, on 8 July, he died from a second attack.[59] Obituaries appeared in major newspapers throughout the South. All the stores in Albany were closed during the hours of his funeral as a sign of mournful respect and tribute for the passing of what the *Atlanta Constitution* described as "one of Albany's most prominent citizens."[60] Condolences poured in from all over the region. The extent of his

October 1877 to 26 December 1879 are known to exist. The issues published during the remaining years of 1880 through 1882 failed to survive.

[56]Albany *Herald*, 8 July 1904; Davis, 25 August 1979.

[57]*History and Reminiscences of Dougherty County*, pp. 200-207.

[58]Letter of Carl F. Lester, 1 February 1978.

[59]Albany *Herald*, 8 July 1904.

[60]Atlanta *Constitution*, 9 July 1904; Savannah *Daily Morning News*, 9 July 1904.

renown was such that notices of his death appeared in German publications.[61] Eulogies and memorial resolutions were read in many B'nai B'rith and Masonic lodges in the South. The depth of the feelings for Charles Wessolowsky and the position of dignity he had achieved among those with whom he came in contact perhaps was expressed best in the eulogy that appeared in the 1904 minutes of the Grand Lodge of Georgia:

> He was truly a man among men, a giant in intellect, with a heart as tender as a woman's and with an energy tireless and indomitable. Coming from a foreign land, he soon learned to admire and love American institutions, and became a patriot sincere and true. By sheer force of character and ability, he rose from humble beginnings to a position of power and dignity in the community. . . . He has left a legacy to his children, to his State and to Masonry—the legacy of an upright life, an untarnished name, and a mind and heart imbued with high and lofty ideals.[62]

Though Charles Wessolowsky left little of material value behind, his legacy to his family and friends was something of greater worth. They inherited from him an optimistic and idealistic outlook on life. "Uncle Charles never stopped saying," reflected Sadie Davis, "that if you are daring enough to touch life you will find that it is good, comforting, and rewarding."[63] The extent of the influence of his outlook could perhaps be measured by the fact that his son Morris had inscribed on his tombstone that very philosophy of life.[64] On his own tombstone, Charles Wessolowsky wanted inscribed his place of birth, the dates of his life and the simple words: "Past Grand High Priest of Georgia." He wanted to be remembered

---

[61] *Beilage zur Allgemeinen Zeitung des Judentums*, 5 August 1904, p. 5.

[62] Excerpts from the Grand Lodge Proceedings for the year 1904 contained in a letter from J.E. Mosely, Worshipful Grandmaster of the Grand Lodge of Georgia, to F. Lamar Pearson of Valdosta, Georgia, 3 February 1978.

[63] Davis, 25 August 1979.

[64] Like his father, Morris Weslosky (he simplified the spelling of his name) is buried at Oakview Cemetery in Albany, Georgia. On his tombstone is inscribed not only a description of his character, but his father's philosophy: "Energetic, cheerful, and able. He touched life at many points and found it good."

for that particular achievement because to him it demonstrated, more than anything else he had accomplished, the extent to which an immigrant Jew living in America, with strength of character and force of will, could enter into brotherhood with his Gentile neighbors and still retain his identity as a Jew and pride in his Jewish heritage.

• Part Two •

The Letters of Charles Wessolowsky
3 March 1878 - 13 October 1879

Letter Number One[1]

Charles Wessolowsky to Rabbi Edward B. M. Browne

Mobile, Alabama
3 March 1878

● ● ●

[*Wessolowsky discusses the B'nai B'rith organization in Uniontown, Alabama, and the value of B'nai B'rith to the survival of American Judaism; praises a Mrs. Ungar of Uniontown not only for her resistance to attempted conversions, but also for the raising of her family in Jewish lore; describes an overnight stay in Demopolis, Alabama, with past Confederate comrades-in-arms; and lauds the Jewish social and cultural life in Mobile, Alabama.*]

● ● ●

Time "flies" slowly on the Alabama Central, and it took a few hours for the noon-train to convey me from Selma to Uniontown. There's something in a name and Uniontown is actually a town of Union, especially insofar as our people are concerned. Messrs. or rather "Brothers" B. Loeway and N. Long, a committee of Concordia Lodge,[2] received me with a brotherly grip and conducted

---

[1]In the course of editing these letters I have corrected misspelled words and modernized some archaic phrases that might cause the reader difficulty. However, where Wessolowsky's spellings, grammar, and punctuations will not cause difficulty, I have preferred to leave his words and style intact. These are, after all, the letters of Wessolowsky and not the editor's. I have added the headings at the beginning of each letter—that is, the writer-recipient designation—to be sure the reader understands that all the letters were written by Wessolowsky to Rabbi Edward Browne. Because not all the letters were dated, and the place of origin was not always indicated, I have added that information (when it was missing) based upon the internal evidence offered in the letters. Finally, in order to provide the reader with the gist of each letter I have added a synopsis of each letter's contents.

[2]Not to be confused with Concordia Lodges, at times called Associations, which were devoted to recreation and social activities. Such lodges usually centered their activities on dramatic performances, literary readings, musical recitals, debates and gala parties. The extent of the activities of each Concordia lodge was obviously dependent upon the size and prosperity of the Jewish community concerned. In any event, such Concordia lodges were to be found only in connection with German-Jewish communities.

me to the residence of M. L. Ernst, Esq., and ere long the benignant smile of my hostess welcomed me as the looked for guest. And there was Mrs. Pake the honored mother of my hostess, and Miss Pake her sister. I am generally very embarassed in the presence of ladies who are stranger to me, but it was made so "home-like" to me, that my blushes grew paler in a short time. Ah, it is so nice to be happy and innocent and blushing. We spent Sunday in visiting the beautiful grounds laid out as the burial place belonging to the Union Hebrew Association.[3] Thus the place of rest for our departed forms, as everywhere, have likewise the first nucleus around which the congregation will crystallize into a future member of the Union of A. H. C.[4]

---

[3]In all their wanderings, the Jews have looked upon the burial ground, or "the house of life" as essential for their collective communal life. It was the focal point of their dearest memories and for that reason the purchase of land for a burial ground gave them a sense of permanency. The desire to purchase land for a cemetery often superseded that of building a synagogue, for religious services could always be held in rented rooms or their homes. The two oldest Jewish cemeteries in the South are located in Charleston (1762) and Savannah (1770). In the 1850s, societies independent of the synagogue were established for the purpose of owning a cemetery, providing grave space and maintaining the plots. The example followed was that set by the congregation Shearith Israel in New York at the end of the 18th century. See Martin Lamm, *The Jewish Way in Death and Mourning* (New York: J. David & Co., 1969).

[4]By the 1850s, the influx of European Jewish immigrants produced a heterogeneous Jewish population of Spanish and Portuguese Jews, Germans, Bohemians, Dutch, French, Polish, and Russians. Each had their own customs and traditions. The differences between these diverse cultures was aggravated by the onset of Reform Judaism. At the same time, there existed pressing needs in areas such as education and self-defense that could only be met by a united Jewry. In 1872, with a donation from Henry Adler of New York, Maritz Loth and Isaac Wise of Cincinnati moved to form a union of American Jewish communities. In July 1873, in Cincinnati, the Union of American Hebrew Congregations came into being, thus becoming the only national religious organization for Jews until the late 1890s. Among its goals was the creation of an organization open to all congregations regardless of theology or religious practice. Its major achievement was the establishment of Hebrew Union College in Cincinnati as a seminary for the training of American Jewish rabbis. See Joseph Buchler, "The Struggle for Unity: Attempts at Union in American Jewish Life," *American Jewish Archives* 2 (1949): 23-25; Steven Fox, "On the Road to Unity: The Union of American Hebrew Congregations and American Jewry, 1873-1903," *American Jewish Archives* 32 (November 1980): 145-93.

The Lodge having extended me the invitation of course, I attended the meeting. I enjoyed the spicy debates and the fine working of our brethren. A wonderful band of Union that B'nai B'rith order! How it tends to make one feel, being a member of Israel's great family. In olden times, before the prayer book was multiplied,[5] the Jew was at home whithersoever he came. No matter though a stranger to all the world when he entered the House of God he was *at home*. The modern tendency of American Judaism, has alienated the Jew from his brother. Every place has another prayer book; you enter a synagogue and you are a stranger. What a sad transformation. Thanks to Providence B.B. Lodge is now the supplement, and no matter where you are, the same work, the same sign, the same spirit, you are *at home* and amongst brothers indeed. After the Lodge I was with my host the whole day receiving calls from the Yehudim [Hebrews] who are numerous.

Monday evening I was escorted to the court house where a very fine audience was assembled, and honored me with their attention to hear what I had to say about "the Jew as a Citizen and Politician."[6] After the lecture a banquet in honor of my humble self,

---

[5]Liturgical reform began in a practical sense with the appearance of alterations in the external aspects of worship in Germany. In 1810, Israel Jacobson created a simplified service for boarding-school children in Essen which he adopted when he became rabbi in Berlin while Isaac Fraenkel and Meyer Bresselau created the Hamburg *Gebetbuch* [prayer book] in 1819 that nurtured the later *Forms of Prayer* written by David Marks in 1841. The German immigrants brought with them these different prayer books to which were added versions reflecting Jewish religious adaptation to the American scene. Among these prayer books were those written by Leo Merzbacher entitled *The Order of Prayer for Divine Service* in 1855, by David Einhorn entitled *Book of Prayers for Israelitsch Congregations* in 1856, and by Isaac Wise entitled *The Daily Prayer Book for American Israelites* in 1857. See Jacob Petuchowski, *Prayer Book Reform in Europe* (New York: World Union for Progressive Judaism, 1968); E. L. Friedland, *Historical and Theological Development of Non-orthodox Jewish Prayerbooks in the United States* (Waltheim, Mass.: Brandeis University, 1967).

[6]In this speech, Wessolowsky reveals his own "pro-Semitic" prejudices. He argued that the moral fiber of the Jew which he derived by his heritage both as a member of the Chosen People and as a persecuted people made him a viable and contributory citizen who takes care of his own and does not need society for his welfare and who seldom commits criminal acts. At the same time, the Jew's propensity for commercial enterprise with the demands on his energies and

at the house of Mrs. Ungar, was tendered me by the citizens of Uniontown. It was a metropolitan sort of thing, with toasts and speeches and good things. We were all ready to do the affair justice.

Mrs. Ungar is one of those ladies whose house is open for all denominations. She has raised many an orphan and relieved many a poor one in the spirit of true charity, unbeknown to the world save through the gratitude of the recipients.

Years ago, when she was the only Jewish resident of Uniontown, the influence of the church and her Christian associates brought all means into requisition to make her forsake her religion, but to no use. Mrs. Ungar remained steadfast in the religion of her fathers and raised a noble family in the same faith all of whom are proud to call her mother.

Tuesday morning, I left Uniontown with a regretful farewell. My thanks are due to the Lodge and all our brethren, but especially to my host and hostess (whom I hope to meet in New Orleans) and to my gallant friend Mr. Leo Proskauker, who was particularly ready in his services. Hope to be in the condition to show my appreciation in future.

Two hours travel brought me to Demopolis, where Messrs. Tannenbaum, Gundesheimer, Levy, and several others met me at the depot, and took me to the house of our mutual friend Tannenbaum, the home of all Shnorrers [chiselers].[7] Friend Tannenbaum is an old soldier of the late unpleasantness, and as leader of a military band, he made music while his brave comrade Jacob Gattman, Esq., now of Aberdeen, carried the standard of the regiment. Music and good humor, and a fine table, a pleasant hostess, a lively host, jovial visitors, what more can one wish for. All of our brethren were very kind to me and especially Mr. Newhouse; who was particularly so. I lectured to a very fine audience at the opera house, and was only sorry that I had to leave Demopolis as soon as next morning.

---

attentions does not allow him the opportunity to enter the demanding and time-consuming profession of politics. See Natchez *Daily Democrat & Courier*, 1 June 1878.

[7]In Yiddish, in which Wessolowsky was fluent, as with other languages, even the most caustic term, if placed in a certain context or uttered with a particular voice inflection, is changed into an endearing term.

I was invited by the Young Men's Hebrew Association[8] to deliver a lecture in New Orleans under their auspices in honor of the Grand Lodge, hence I had, of course, to be in New Orleans at the opening of the session, and was in a hurry. I had to pass Meridian without stopping. At Mobile, I have some old chums whom I have not seen for ever so long, and I concluded to stop over for a few hours. Mobile is a fine city, aristocratic Yehudim [Hebrews], and wealthy ones.[9] I was invited to the play of "Married Life," enacted by the "Fidelia," and it was an actual treat. Had I not been convinced that I was in an amateur theatre, I'd have taken the actors as regular professionals. I will be back in Mobile and give more particulars about it, but must mention the pleasant surprise of presenting a gold-headed cane (between the acts) to Mr. Solomon, for 15 years the dramatic director of the society. Mr. S. Haas, the orator of the society, wherever eloquence is called for, made the presentation address. I had the honor of meeting the Hon. A. Proskauer (Major Proskauer) and Hon. Nat Straus, brother of the Hon. Isidor Straus, two of the leading citizens here, and spent much of my time in company with Rev. Dr. Moses,[10] whose acquaintance gives me much pleasure. Dr. Moses is one of those men who work hard for their congregation as well as for their own store of information without "puffing" their efforts. And he is very much beloved by the congregation in turn. Have received several invitations, asking me to take my tour from New Orleans up the

---

[8]The Y. M. H. A. is the predecessor to the Jewish Community Center. It was created to perpetuate Judaism through a program of recreation and education in Jewish culture much like the Y. M. C. A. after which it was patterned. The Y. M. H. A. traces its origin to the Jewish literary societies established in the 1840s. The first Y. M. H. A. was established in Baltimore in 1854.

[9]Mobile is one of the few Southern Jewish communities about which anything has been written. For a brief, but inadequate glimpse at the Jewish community in Mobile, see Bertram Korn, *The Jews of Mobile, Alabama, 1763-1841* (Cincinnati: American Jewish Archives, 1970).

[10]Wessolowsky's use of the Christian term, "reverend," is indicative of one of the slow processes of evolution of any immigrant minority. Namely, while trying to retain the inner meaning of the values which were brought over from the old country, acculturalization first occurs by utilizing the terminology of the surrounding majority. In this manner, an attempt is tried to either minimize the danger generated by outward difference or to maximize basic similarities.

Mississippi, but time will control all my movements. I leave for New Orleans in an hour.

W.

[At the beginning, Wessolowsky ended his letters with his one initial, "W."; later—see letter number eight—he began using "C.W."]

Letter Number Two

Charles Wessolowsky to Rabbi Edward B. M. Browne

Selma, Alabama
26 April 1878

• • •

[*Wessolowsky meets with the Jewish residents of Cuthbert, Georgia, on his way to Eufaula, Alabama; describes the good relations that exist between Jew and Gentile in that town; notes the active social life in Selma, Alabama, that revolves around the Harmony Club; mentions the prominent economic and political positions held by the Jews of Selma.*]

• • •

Having concluded to attend the meeting of the Grand Lodge of District No. 7,[11] at New Orleans, several Lodges and Congregations whom information to that effect seems to have reached, did me the honor of inviting me to lecture before them, and having a few days of leisure I accepted some of those brotherly calls. The first place on my road was Eufaula, Ala. I left my home in the company of Mr. Emanuel (whom the people of Macon at the last Jewish Fair,[12]

---

[11]On the national level, B'nai B'rith was divided, unlike the Masonic lodges after which it modeled itself, into multi-state regional districts. The administrative structure of each district was called the Grand Lodge of District so-and-so. District No. 5, for example, of which Wessolowsky was Grand Vice-President included the states of Georgia, North Carolina, South Carolina, Virginia, Maryland and the District of Columbia. District No. 7 included Alabama, Mississippi, Tennessee, Louisiana, Arkansas, Florida, and Texas.

[12]The so-called "Jewish Fair," was a technique whereby the Jewish community, usually under the sponsoring of the women of the community, would raise money for a variety of purposes. These "fairs," which Wessolowsky will have other occasions to mention, were a reflection of the growing stature of women in the vitality and activity of the Jewish communities. The monies gathered from these bazaars went for building funds, charitable activities, upkeep of existing structures, etc. The "fairs" were similar to the county fairs and in some towns became quite popular. The "Jewish fairs" were always open to the public, Jew and Gentile alike, and frequently were capped with a gala evening ball or dance.

distinguished as the most popular gentleman) and reached Cuthbert where I had the pleasure of being intercepted at the depot by my friends Messrs. E. Pulaske and P. Harris, who insisted upon my stopping over in their city; but of course having been announced for that very evening for a lecture at Eufaula I had to deny myself the pleasure of a nice time with the Israelites of Cuthbert, and obeying the "all aboard" I stepped into the car. On my arrival at Eufaula I was met by a committee consisting of Messrs. H. Bernstein (President), E. Kuttner and G. D. Stern, and before long I actually found myself *at home* in Mr. Bernstein's interesting family. The afternoon was devoted to visiting the bluff, one of the most delightful spots—a natural park. In the evening, I had the pleasure to address the citizens on "the Jew as a Citizen and Politician." It is not for me to say that the audience was pleased with me, but so much is certain, that I was charmed by my audience. The lecture over, a reception at Mr. Bernstein's followed where music, wit and wine sparkled in all abundance. It was one of those social reunions which characterize people. It was midnight or possibly a little beyond, when we dispersed.

Eufaula boasts many fine buildings but especially grand church edifices. Show me a city with fine churches and I will show you an intelligent community. Our brethren here have been imbued with a sense of more than mere duty and succeeded in purchasing a church which was converted into a synagogue,[13] and a very fine one at that

---

[13]The synagogue, literally meaning "place of assembly," probably originated during the period of the Babylonian Captivity and slowly became the social and religious center by the first century c.e. It is to be distinguished from the Great Temple in Jerusalem in that it was a multi-purpose structure beyond the sole requirements of religious worship. It was a school, social hall, meeting place and house of prayer wrapped up into one. It contained no sacred ground. During the Middle Ages, all daily life was involved in the synagogue. In the 18th century, Orthodox congregations built synagogues or adapted existing structures with separate seating or galleries for women. Salaried officiants led the service and a great emphasis was placed on decorum in the religious service. The Hasidic synagogues, on the other hand, eliminated pews and salaried officiants. The internal appearance was austere and the service was informal with the congregants leading their own service. The synagogue, whatever the variation of design, had to meet certain requirements: it had to have windows; the ark had to be on the east side of the building and the entrance doors on the west side; until recently, the Torah had to be read from a platform in the center of the sanctuary.

considering their number. I had the pleasure to become acquainted with several prominent Christians amongst them the Rev. Mr. Gregory of the First Baptist Church, a profound scholar.

Mr. Gregory showed me all around in his beautiful church gotten up in metropolitan style. It would grace a square in Atlanta. (Our chief while here lectured in that church.)[14] I will mention the beautiful study for the minister and a grand library all the property of the congregation. How rarely do we find a Jewish congregation thinking of their ministers' comfort in building a temple.[15] Let us take lessons in that respect from our Christian neighbors, who provide dwellings and studies for their pastor. I left Eufaula after spending another pleasant day with my friends, old and new, who will please accept the assurance of my full appreciation of their various favors.

And now permit me to ask you the question, have you ever traveled in a chicken-coop? Well, if you did, it will not be strange for you to know what I felt on taking a box-car on the night train for Selma. Oh, it was grand. The finest sleeping car out. I made myself as comfortable as the geese our ladies fatten for Pesach,[16] and

---

[14]The "chief" to whom Wessolowsky refers is Rabbi Edward Browne.

[15]With the Reform movement, the synagogue became an elaborate, dignified and lavishly furnished structure. Most reform synagogues were built solely for the purpose of worship. Hence, reform Jews preferred to call their synagogue "temple." It thus became permissible for the Jews to purchase a Christian church without compromising their belief that their house of worship had to have been from the moment of conception nothing other than a house of worship. Inside the temple, the ark and pulpit were elaborate edifices. The pews were arranged in straight rows with no special separate section for women. The officiants were salaried officials of the congregation. In general, the architecture of the temples was highly influenced in style and internal arrangement by existing Christian churches.

[16]*Pesach* (pronounced pay-sak) is the Hebrew word for the Jewish celebration of Passover which commemorates the Jewish exodus from Egypt. The most renowned characteristic of the holiday is the *matzos* (pronounced mah-tzoes) or unleavened bread. It is a joyous holiday in which God's covenant with the Jews is acknowledged and the freedom of the Jews is celebrated. The holiday is marked by a week-long preparation in which the Jewish home is expunged of all foods containing any leavening. Separate dishes and flatware are also used which have not been touched by any leavening. The traditional meal centers around a fattened goose, the fat of which is used to make *schmalz*, a cooking fat, and the feathers from which find their way into pillows, mattresses, and blankets. The ritual meal was the *seder* (pronounced say-dah) at which the story of the exodus is retold.

intended to embark in a good long sleep, when lo and behold! In comes a lady. Well, that did not frighten me, but she had a little babe in her arms, and what a voice! (I mean the babe not the lady.) It took me nearly all night to ascertain who was the composer of that terribly sweet music, which possesses many charms for me and animates my soul and body so that it kept me awake all night—Mr. Editor I am yet at a loss to find out the name of the composer, and must be satisfied with the conviction, that as all babes are angels that it must have been heavenly music, perhaps prompted by Gabriel's trumpet. But enough—I reached Selma at 10 o'clock a.m., and had the pleasure of traveling with Col. Sandford of Montgomery, who came over to Selma as the orator at the decoration of the graves of our Confederate dead.

I had concluded not to lecture in Selma by reason of the "Memorial Day," but stopped over anyway to meet some of our chief's friends in Selma, he speaks of so frequently as a set of people especially "young" and intelligent in every respect.

Having dropped in without notice of course I was my own committee and hurried to Mr. A. Meyers' store in order to receive the letters our chief promised us, but I was sadly disappointed. While turning round to leave the place, a tall blonde with open face and blue eyes emerged from the rear of the department and asked me in a pleasant alto "Are you Senator Wessolowsky?" Of course I could not deny myself and ere long I was in possession of the looked for letter from home, and acquainted with the young lady, who is one of our chief's Montgomery "Girls" now here on a visit in company of two other young ladies, Misses Nannie Weil and Bertha Rice. I was very much satisfied with my Post Office and Miss Milvenah Jacobi, my kind Post mistress, and promised myself a pleasant time at the Harmony Club[17] entertainment given tonight in honor of the Montgomery guests to which I am invited.—I strolled about Selma and met our brethren and was convinced that the Selma Israelites will sustain their reputation as true.

---

[17]The Harmony Clubs were social and entertainment groups designed to maintain a cohesion among the German Jews in a community. At times, they were alternatives to the Concordia Clubs. At other times, they were successors to Concordia.

They seem to be in good circumstances, and are doing the largest business in the city. They are highly respected by our Gentile friends, and two of these Messrs. A. Kayser and Joy Mayer, are members of the City Council. The former was repeatedly honored on various occasions, so that he represented the Mayor at the time His Highness King Frog took charge of the city, and also made the presentation speech in behalf of the Fire Company, of which he is a member; to the foreman who sometime ago was honored by his Company in presenting him a silver set, and well did he acquit himself of the task imposed upon him. We bespeak for him a brilliant future career.

We had also met to our greatest delight our old friend "Hank Rosenbaum," who with his popularity, liberality and ease, has gained a host of friends amongst Jew and Gentile, and rendered good services to *Jewish South*—for which I will thank your brother Hank, and promise at your wedding to reciprocate—or if you desire select the one for you.

The Harmony Club sociable was brilliant, an array of young folks in number and culture worthy of a city like Atlanta. The young men especially attentive and liberal. I met Miss Weil (your "pet" school girl of ten years ago I learn now a bloomy maiden), and Miss Rice. Miss Jacobi was absent, being in mourning for her brother Silvey. Our friend Hank was jolly and happy with the rest, and who could help in the midst of such beautiful ladies. (Don't tell my wife on me.)

If the Harmony Club is a beautiful social center, you can rest assured that the religious focus of Judaism was not neglected by our people here. The Episcopalians having built a new church, our brethren procured and paid for the old church, which has been transformed into a temple.[18] It is a beautiful structure with a capacity of eight hundred souls. Our chief lectured in that building

---

[18]It was not uncommon for a Jewish community on the verge of constructing a place of worship to purchase an old church building and renovate it. This practice was particularly true of the reform-oriented congregation since most churches met most of the requirements for a "temple" even if it was facing in the wrong direction. In any event, this practice of securing a house of worship was cheaper, faster and

three times, only a year ago, preaching the confirmation sermon[19] on Shevuos.[20] Rev. G. L. Rosenberg, late of Montgomery, a very excellent chazan[21] and teacher is the minister, and gives general satisfaction. I met here with Mr. Louis Gerstman (brother of the well-known Reverend from St. Joseph, Mo.), engaged in the Insurance business, an acquaintance of mine whom I have lost sight of some twelve years ago. He is doing right well.

In conclusion, let me say that they have here a Jewish hotel, Mrs. Schuster, proprietress, which is one of the finest houses in the

---

less agonizing than constructing one from the ground up.

[19]The confirmation ceremony was first introduced by Israel Jacobson in Germany at the beginning of the nineteenth century as a substitute for *Bar Mitzvah* (pronounced bar-mitts-vah and means "son of the commandment.") The ceremony is held at a later age than that of the traditional thirteen for *Bar Mitzvah* on the grounds that before that age a person cannot understand the meaning of the ritual in which he is participating and the responsibility involved with being received as an adult into the community. By the end of the 19th century, in the United States, confirmation had been adopted as a ceremony in addition to *Bar Mitzvah* and was associated with the conclusion of Sunday School attendance. The ceremony is usually held around *Shevuos*. The confirmant recites various selections from Scripture and declares a devotion to Judaism.

[20]*Shevuos* or *Shabuoth* (pronounced sha-vu-ohs) means "Feast of Weeks." It falls just seven weeks after Passover. It is one of the pilgrimage festivals, for it is both a holiday of the first fruits and the time of the giving of the Torah by God to Moses on Mount Sinai. *Shevuos* is the middle of the "Three Festivals" of Passover, *Shevuos* and *Succos* or *Sukkoth* (pronounced sue-kos) meaning Tabernacles. Like the other two festivals the holiday is one of joy and thanksgiving commemorating the kind deeds God did in redeeming the Jews from Egypt, giving them the Torah, settling them in the Promised Land and teaching them the true ways of life. This holiday, like the other two, though perhaps nationalistic in aspiration, is imbued with universal human hopes and religious ideas: liberty (Passover); revelation (*Shevuos*); thanksgiving (*Succos*).

[21]Originally the *chazan* or *hayan* (pronounced ha-zahn), was a caretaker of the synagogue and a functionary at religious ceremonies. During the Middle Ages he officiated in synagogue services. In modern times, he is the cantor who chants the religious services at temples and synagogues.

country for a regular kosher meal.[22] Let all our readers patronize Mrs. S., when in Selma.

W.

---

[22]*Kosher* (pronounced ko-shur) literally means "fit" or "proper." The term refers to the Jewish laws and customs pertaining to the types of food permitted for consumption and after proper preparation. All fruits may be eaten. The Holy Scripture separates animals into clean and unclean categories. The clean animals must be ritually slaughtered in a manner that is merciful and painless and that allows all blood to be expunged from the carcass. The slaughtering, therefore, is done with a ritual knife by a ritual slaughterer called a *shochet* or *shohet* (pronounced show-chet with a gutteral -ch) who is employed by the congregation. The essence of the slaughter is the slitting of the throat and draining of all blood. It is not permissible to use the hindquarter unless veins are removed. Sick animals are unclean. Fish with scales and fins may be eaten while shellfish, scaleless fish, reptiles, insects, etc., are forbidden. Historically, these laws were extremely important in giving identity to the Jewish people. Their observance, however, prevented the Jews from intermingling freely with Gentiles. Consequently, one of the first rituals to suffer the effects of acculturation in the United States or the earlier reform movement in Germany was the observance of the dietary laws.

Letter Number Three

Charles Wessolowsky to Rabbi Edward B. M. Browne

Baton Rouge, Louisiana
25 May 1878

• • •

[*Wessolowsky describes the religious activities of the Jewish community in Donaldsonville, Louisiana; travels to Plaquemine, Louisiana, where he likewise applauds the labors of the Jewish residents "for the good and noble principles" of Judaism; In Natchez, Mississippi, he writes in detail of the activities and leadership of Samuel Ullman, editor of the* Natchez Democrat & Sun; *discusses both the business success of Natchez Jewry and its religious unity; mentions the Jewish residents of Fayette, Mississippi, as he passes through the town; and lectures in Rodney, Mississippi, to both the Jewish and Gentile residents.*]

• • •

We left New Orleans Tuesday morning en route for Donaldsonville, and landed at our place of destination about noon. There we handed our letters of introduction to Messrs. Loeb and Klappman, and soon found ourselves again in the hands of good and worthy conductors; we formed the acquaintance of Mr. A. Levy, who has shown us a great deal of courtesy and attention, and to whom the *Jewish South* is indebted for new subscribers.

Now, Mr. Editor, Donaldsonville is a small place, about 2,000 inhabitants, in the sugar bowl of Louisiana, and is one of the most flourishing little cities in the state, and, as usual, our brethren have the sway of the business, and are doing well; but they are not alone doing well in a material point, they are not alone endeavoring to accumulate riches and wealth, but also in religion and training of their children, thus they have built a handsome synagogue, wherein they hold their regular Sabbath worship and conduct their services, under the leadership of Rev. Dr. Sophar, to the honor and credit of Judaism.[23] Their business places are closed night and morning

---

[23]The standards and criteria by which Wessolowsky judged these Jewish

during service hours. Their choir, consisting of volunteers, are indeed deserving of great praise for their energy and efficiency. The synagogue in Donaldsonville, as well as in other places, had been built through the efforts and perseverance of our Jewish ladies.[24] In Donaldsonville the ladies a few years ago gave a ball and a fair which realized six thousand dollars, and which money was promptly turned over for the building and outfitting of a synagogue. The officers of the Congregation are: Mr. G. Fidel, President; W. Klappman, V. P.; and A. Levi, Secretary.

A Ladies' Hebrew Benevolent Society is also here, and in a flourishing condition.[25] Mrs. Weinschenk is President; Mrs. B.

communities were the same values by which he lived and the same demands he made of himself. His pride in economic success and respect for cultural activity within the communities he visited and observed are muted if such accomplishments were not utilized to augment the religious life of the community. He reserved his greatest applause and most caustic comments as he observed the religious activities of these communities. Wherever he traveled, he looked for the watchtowers of his faith: a synagogue in which the community worshipped; a Hebrew Benevolent Society through which the community carried out its charitable responsibilities; a fraternal lodge with which a sense of brotherhood was forged; a Sunday School in which the children were educated in the ways of their forefathers. The decibel level of his applause was proportional not only to the existence of these institutions, but according to their activity. Conversely, his applause for the existence and operation of these institutions was balanced by quiet admonishments in the absence of some. His anger boiled up, however, in those communities where the Jewish religious structures, social organizations, and fraternal lodges were not to be found.

[24]One of the yet-untold stories of the impact of the immigration of Jews to American on their social institutions is that of the changing role women played in the American Jewish communities and the functioning of the synagogue. Faced with problems of economic and cultural adjustment, it was impossible for the men in the community to shoulder alone the whole burden of establishing and maintaining the community. The women usually were instrumental first in fundraising to purchase a cemetery or to construct a house of worship, and to assume the responsibility of its upkeep. In addition, with the advent of Sunday School as a replacement of the *cheder* or *heder* (pronounced chay-der with a gutteral -ch) and the need for lay teachers, the women's home role of teaching children became a communal one. Much of this change in communal role may have had an influence on and acted as a constant pressure to equalize institutional attitudes such as separating men and women in religious services and on social occasions.

[25]While the original social and charitable organizations were male-organized and dominated, in small communities such as those in the South the absence of available manpower required the involvement of women, and that they form their own such organizations.

Lehman, Treasurer; and Mrs. Blum, Secretary.

The Rev. Dr. Sophar, we admire for his candor and truthfulness towards us. He is a polished and intelligent gentleman, and we were delighted in forming his acquaintance. He, with Mr. A. Levy, accompanied us until nearly time for the departure of the boat for the next place, and at four o'clock a.m., we bade adieu to Donaldsonville and embarked for Plaquemine, where we arrived about eleven o'clock. On the steamer we met Mr. Meyer Michael, from Waterloo, and also Mr. D. Levi, from Plaquemine, who are great admirers of the *Jewish South*. We met Mr. Kowalski, who was kind enough to give us his assistance in bringing us to Mr. Leon Meyer, the President of the Congregation. We met Dr. Lehman, "our mutual friend," who took charge of us, and has shown us the interesting places of Plaquemine, of which, foremost stands the little, neatly-fitted-up synagogue, which, as yet, has not been dedicated. We formed the acquaintance of all our Israelitish brethren, and were very much pleased with the little city. We met also, Mr. Schenks, the editor of the "Iberville South," who is a jovial and pleasing gentleman, and to whom we are under obligations for courtesies extended us. After partaking of supper with the President, Secretary and Treasurer of the congregation—"*Lovers of Peace*"— we remained in the company of the Doctor, whose eloquence and interesting conversation kept us awake until three o'clock, the time when we have to take the steamer for Baton Rouge. To the Doctor and all the Israelites of Plaquemine, we extend our hearty thanks for kindness shown to us. Our thanks are also due to Mr. Leon Myers in whose house we spent a delightful evening, and who, with his musical talent assisted by Miss Kowalski (a very fine performer on the piano), succeeded in entertaining us most pleasantly and we all regretted when the time came for our departure. The energy of the Israelites in Plaquemine will bring success to the congregation, which is young and few in number. Through the efforts of Mr. Kowalski and the doctor, the Jewish children are receiving instructions in the faith of our ancestors, and if we mistake not, Dr. Lehman is the superintendent of the Sabbath-school. May they forever energetically continue in their labors for the good and noble principles of our religion.

Time rolled by. We departed for Baton Rouge, where we arrived at six o'clock a.m., and were the guest of Mr. Block.

In our last we announced our arrival at Natchez, where we were the guest of Mr. and Mʀs. Loevenberg, who, with their general hospitality and full attention to our comforts and wants, made our stay very pleasant and agreeable. We found opportunity of speaking of Georgia very frequently as the Solomons of Savannah, Mrs. Hyam of Augusta, Alexander of Atlanta, all relatives of our worthy hostess, and all of whom we have the good fortune to know.

In starting out to visit our brethren, of course the first with whom we shook hands was our mutual friend S. Ullman, the popular and famous gentleman of Natchez, and well does he deserve the epitaph heaped upon him by a gentleman in New Orleans, by naming him the type of kindness and generosity, the picture of true and noble manhood.

He was very glad to see us, and we of course, not less. He offered his regrets at our not being his guests, as Mrs. Ullman was on a visit to New Orleans. We regret exceedingly at not having made her acquaintance. We assured him that we were pleasantly, aye, very pleasantly quartered, only regretting that Mrs. Ullman was indisposed, for which reason she was compelled to consult a physician. We started on, observing the various attractions of Natchez and receiving introductions to Jews and Gentiles—whose acquaintance we were proud to make. Our first visit was directed to the house of Rev. Mr. Rosenfield, whom we found to be an intelligent and polished scholar, well worth and deserving the function he occupies. The Rev. treated us very kindly, and will ever be remembered as an able representative of Judaism. We then proceeded to pay our repects to the editors and associates of the *Natchez Democrat* and the *Sun*, whom we found to be accomplished and social gentlemen, ready to hear and give a good joke at any time.

May the "Democrat" waive long and the "Sun" shed his lustre and brilliant light upon his readers to many years to come. If you will not reveal the secret, we will tell you that our honorable contributor,[26] Mr. Ullman is one of the editors, and you know, that "his quill is mightier than the sword," and that it adds but renown

---

[26]Much of the local news published in the *Jewish South* was sent to Atlanta by solicited volunteer "stringers" who frequently dispatched their news under imaginative pen names.

and fame to any paper where his articles appear. "Onward" was the cry, and although our guide was receiving the full benefit of a hot May noon's sun, still he was willing and ready to bring us to all our brothers, and we soon found ourselves in a circle of Jehudim [Hebrews] and enjoying the pleasure of our new acquaintances, until the time came when we had to prepare for our lecture that evening.

At a quarter past eight we were conducted into the gorgeous and handsome temple by the President of the congregation,[27] Mr. Ullman, and our noble host and hostess. There we met a very fair and numerous audience assembled to honor us by hearing what we had to say, and again the Jew was shown up in his true standing as a citizen, which, if we mistake not, met with the approval of Jew and Gentile. We are thankful to our friend Ullman, for the novel and flattering introduction given us. Rest assured brother Ullman, we appreciate it. We then returned to "Our Home," enjoying the sparkling wine in the company of many visitors, among them we had the pleasure of meeting the accomplished and highly intelligent Mrs. Frank, whom undoubtedly our editor-in-chief well remembers, and who deserves a special mention for her zeal and energetic endeavors in teaching a class in the Sabbath school. Nature reminded us of our duty, and we soon found ourselves in the arms of Morpheus, dreaming of all that was so pleasing to the mind and eye during the day and evening.

The following day again brought us to the "All Man" (Ullman), and we were out on a mission for the *Jewish South*—which, thanks to the popularity and endeavors of our guide and friend, soon found itself successful.

Natchez is one of the most handsome and beautiful cities in Mississippi, and can boast of great enterprises, seldom to be found in any other place south. Among others we notice a large cotton factory, producing various cotton cloths, equal to any made North or South; and which articles, we understand are now finding ready sale in the markets of St. Louis and elsewhere. Through the

---

[27]Congregation literally means "assembly," and while such a word is often employed in Christianity to refer to the members of a specific Protestant sect, in Judaism it refers to the social and sacral Jewish community. That is, it has a specific reference to the dues-paying members associated with the institution of the temple administration as well as to the Jewish community as a whole.

kindness of Mr. Frank, we had an opportunity of examining his mammoth building and stock of dry goods, boots and shoes, etc., kept by him for wholesale trade only, and which will favorably compare with any stock in the city of New Orleans and other places. There are also other large business firms as G. A. Jacobs, our host Mr. Loevenberg and others, too numerous to mention. In all, our brothers here are, as usual doing the largest business of the place, and are doing well.

Here in this part of Mississippi, and in the "sugar bowl" of Louisiana, we find the dream of our friend, Mr. Eichberg, of Atlanta, realized. Our Israelites are drifting strongly toward being agriculturists, and a great many of them have a plantation of their own, and are rentors [landlords], and thus reproducing the occupation of our ancestors, and which seems to be to them a very prosperous business.[28]

The congregation in Natchez, with their beautiful temple—S. Ullman as President, S. Schatz Vice President, and Rev. Dr. Rosenfeld as their spiritual guide, seems to prosper very much. We cannot refrain from mentioning that more unity, concert of action and harmony does not exist in a stronger term and measure anywhere than it does among the Israelites of this city, who number about forty families. We wish them, in the language of Rip Van Winkle, "may they live long and prosper."

Scarcity of time compelled us to move on to Fayette, regretting exceedingly we did not have the opportunity of hearing their splendid choir, which, as we understand, is the finest in the city. But, if the nightingale, Miss _____ opposite our hostess, is a fair specimen of the voices composing the choir, and whose clear and ringing voice we had the pleasure to hear, whose sweet and melodious notes charmed our soul, we do not doubt the verdict that it is fine, superb, aye, heavenly. We sometimes, even now, imagine hearing her thrilling voice.

---

[28]As Wessolowsky indicates, the ownership and working of the land forged a link among Jews, at least he thought it should, with the agricultural heritage of ancient Israel and created a spiritual and prideful union with the past. In addition, such ownership was a vivid reminder of the freedoms enjoyed by Jews in America in sharp contrast to the prohibitions experienced by friends and family in Europe.

The Sabbath school is superintended by the minister, aided ably by Mrs. Ullman and Mrs. Frank and others, whose names we have not learned. But enough, we could fill the columns with items from Natchez, but must away and bid adieu to the worthy host, hostess, and their interesting family. We were conveyed to the depot in the private equipage [carriage] of Mr. Loevenberg, and boarded the train for Fayette, the brother of our host accompanying us, and we soon found ourselves comfortably seated, meditating over all that has transpired within the past few days.

At six o'clock Friday evening, we landed at Fayette; went immediately to Messrs. Eiseman & Son, to whom we had a letter of introduction, so kindly given to us by Mr. Loevenberg. There we were hospitably received, and these gentlemen have done all in their power to offer us aid and assistance in procuring conveyance to Rodney and in behalf of the "South." We remained in their house until Saturday evening, enjoying the kind treatment and hospitality extended by Mrs. Eiseman, senior and junior, the latter being a daughter of our friend Mr. Joseph of New Orleans, and here again we spoke of those relatives of Georgia, until our conveyance was before the door.

We soon started off for Rodney—a distance of about sixteen miles, in a carriage consisting of a locomotive power, represented by Belam on his journey, and the vehicle, which although gave us an elevated position, yet must have been saved by Noah and preserved in his ark—as antiquity was stamped on its face, and indeed we revere it for the sake of its ancient and oriental appearance—praying at the same time, "O Lord deliver us from temptation." We passed over a very hilly country and reached Rodney about four hours from the time of leaving Fayette. Here we were the guest of Mr. and Mrs. Haas, to whom we were introduced by the courtesy of Mrs. Eiseman, and again we were made to feel at home. We remained at Rodney, a small city of a few hundred inhabitants, until Tuesday—in the meantime, crossing the river over to the Louisiana side, visiting St. Joseph, of which city and Israelites we will speak in our next, as we promised to return that next Sunday to participate in the deliberation of their meetings in the lodge of I.O.B.B. [International Order of B'nai B'rith].

Monday night, having been requested by all Israelites, and some Gentiles, residing at Rodney, to lecture there, and the Presbyterian church having been offered for that purpose, we could not decline, and although it being but a small city, yet the audience was very fair and appreciative.

Tuesday morning, after taking leave of the Haas family, and all, particularly of our friend Mr. Baum, whose courtesy and kindness will long be remembered, we started in a fine equipage, tendered us by the Israelites of Rodney, for Port Gibson, where we arrived in due time, a distance of about twenty miles, again traveling over hilly country, which reminded us of the destiny of the human kind, as *up* we climbed very slowly, cautiously, and with all force endeavoring to reach the top of the hill, the highest pinnacle, and yet hardly had we ascended the same than *downward* was our road and in a much quicker speed, and with more swiftness than we had ascended; for the reason that horses, wagon, in fact, everything and everybody is only too glad to help us down, either smoothly, or, if necessary, kick us down. Is this not so? We think it is a true picture of life, and it struck us very forcibly.

Here we must stop—will give you outlines of Port Gibson in our next epistle. *Au revoir.*

W.

Letter Number Four

Charles Wessolowsky to Rabbi Edward B. M. Browne

Farmersville, Mississippi
June 1878

● ● ●

[*Wessolowsky describes a murder case involving local Jewish residents of Port Gibson, Mississippi, and how justly they were treated; discusses the activities of B'nai B'rith Lodge in Port Gibson and the lecture he gave at the Odd Fellows Hall; at St. Joseph, Louisiana, he met Jewish residents from the surrounding small towns such as Waterproof, Louisiana, commenting on their prominent social and political positions in such towns; and of the Monroe, Louisiana, Jewish community he is highly critical of their religious disinterest although they possess an active B'nai B'rith Lodge.*]

● ● ●

Arrived at Port Gibson, we soon found ourselves in the hands of friends, and hospitalities were lavishly bestowed upon us by Messr. L. Newman, of the firm of L. Kiefer & Co., and our young friend, Mr. G. Gunst, whom we knew when he resided in Georgia and others. Mr. Kahn and family made our stay comfortable and pleasant. The city was somewhat in a state of excitement and very busy, as old and young were constantly engaged in courting (not the ladies) but the stern and learned Judge (the Circuit Court being in session) and jurors. Witnesses and officers of the court were seen running to and from the court house, answering to the sounds of the bell, or to the calling of their names, fearing their pockets may be made lighter by the decree of the Judge, who, we understand, was determined to enforce the rules of court, and make the sons of Ham, who play a very conspicuous part in the courts of Mississippi (as there are ten colored and two white jurors) as well as others do their duty. A great interest was manifested by the citizens in various murder cases, in which our co-religionists also displayed a vast amount of feeling, as in one case the murderer and in another the murdered party were Israelites. We were presnt at the trial for bail of the party who was charged with murder, and we are happy to state that the honest, impartial and learned Judge, released him on the small amount of two hundred and fifty dollars bail, believing that the killing was without any malice, and entirely in self-defense. We were proud to see that honesty, uprightness and impartiality were so strongly exhibited by the Judges in the various courts which we had the occasion to witness and that matters seem to assume a more calm and quiet attitude in Mississippi.

Our Israelitish brethren are very much respected, they are carrying on the largest business houses as L. Kiefer & Co., Wm. Kahn, and others, are a pride to any community, and no doubt give evidence of the prosperity of the city.

There is a B'nai B'rith Lodge here in a very flourishing condition, and a Sabbath-school, in which our friend, Mr. Picard, and Miss Kiefer, the talented young lady who lately has won so many laurels for herself in the art of performing on the piano in the city of New Orleans, where she participated in a concert given for some charitable purpose, take a great deal of interest, they being the teachers, and energetically looking after promoting the cause of Judaism in this particular.

We are indebted to Mr. A. Trutsch and friend Gunst, for courtesies bestowed upon us and to the *Jewish South,* as through the aid of those gentlemen we received many new subscribers.

Friday night we lectured in Odd Fellows' Hall[29] to a very fair audience. We were at all times inspired by the warmth and lustre of the forever shining "Sun" [the Natchez newspaper, the *Sun*] which is indeed worthy of notice, as Port Gibson is the only place where the "Sun" never sets, having seen him shining brightly at ten and eleven o'clock at night. Go on in your good work, brother *Sun,* and you will soon see and feel that others are not less inspired nor pleased by the rays of the lights.

---

[29]The Odd Fellows originated in eighteenth-century England. The first American lodge was organized in Baltimore in 1819 and maintained ties with the parent order in England. The separation between American and English orders came in 1843. The purpose of this order was to aid and comfort its members and their families. Its logo speaks of friendship, love and truth while reminding the members of human mortality and divine omnipresence. The Odd Fellows served as one of the major models for the formation of such Jewish social organizations as B'nai B'rith.

Saturday morning we took the train for Grand Gulf, there to embark for St. Joseph, which place we reached after two hours' ride on the steamer, and met Mr. B. Levy at the wharf, awaiting our arrival, and he conducted us to his house, where we met with a hearty welcome. We spent Saturday in making acquaintances of Jew and Gentile, introduced by our friend, Mr. Sachse, the popular Israelite of St. Joe , and Sunday morning we met the brothers from Waterproof Lake, St. Joe and Rodney, assembled in the Lodge room of the I.O.B.B., where we spoke upon the aims and objects of the Order, and enjoyed our new acquaintances; particularly the Hon. A. G. Yamer, the Mayor of Waterproof. He is well worthy, and indeed, a pride of Judaism. Mr. Sachse is President of the School Board of the Parish, and the office could not have been given in better hands, and could not have been bestowed upon any one who works more zealously, energetically and truthfully in the cause of education. He is a very polished scholar and is very much respected by his Gentile friends for his honesty and integrity in all his dealings and doings with mankind. If we mistake not in the signs of the times, his voice will soon be heard in the legislative halls of Louisiana. I bespeak for him in advance, success in any career of life he might be placed in, and we know well that Judaism will be honored by his efforts and elevated by his station. To my friend, Mr. Levy, who so energetically labored in behalf of the *Jewish South*, obtaining many Gentile subscribers, and who is a gentleman of the first order, we return our thanks. His courtesies will forever remain fresh in our memory, and we will be only too proud if we can be of any service to him in the future. The Israelites here are enjoying a very good reputation; some of them are Aldermen of the city, and seem to do very well. We only regret that we did not meet the Dryfus family, they having left just as we landed.

Monday morning, we bade adieu to St. Joe, and to our friends who accompanied us to the steamer, and off we went for Vicksburg. There we arrived in the evening, made the acquaintance of the Rev. Dr. Gotthelf and other gentlemen, and concluded to go over to Monroe and other cities in Northern Louisiana and then return here. Thus we started Tuesday across to the Louisiana side, took the train for Monroe, and soon found ourselves before the door of our friend, J. S. Kaliski, who, with his usual hospitality and renowned kindness, bestowed upon us everything that made us feel "home, home again."

We started out in company with our friend to give greetings to our brethren, and we found them to be a clever set, fully endowed with the whim for business, and enwrapped strictly so in this cause. They boast of a nice temple, but *of what avail?*

No minister, no one from whose lips is heard expounding the word of God, and thus the temple stands, magnificent in its structure, grand in its appearance, until the time arrives when our co-religionists, either for fear, or habit and custom, see fit, at least, to keep three holy days in the year.[30] There are but few members belonging to the congregation, and there seems to be a lukewarmness displayed by some of our Yehudim [Hebrews] in Monroe in behalf of the cause which we regretted very much to see. Our brethren, if united, are well able to support a minister, and could obtain one easily, if not too much is asked of him for the salary paid. Not every one can be a Demosthenes, and not all can be a Socrates, and would they be, perhaps, then, they would not find favor for reason he is not a fine singer, or chazan [synagogue cantor].

We were induced to say this much, as we believe from eye observation, and inquiry that there are a few among our co-religionists in Monroe, who are so indifferent, so careless in the true cause of our religion that they indeed are an obstacle in the path of those who are anxious and desirous of promoting and elevating our holy cause, and to those, our few words, we trust, will not be amiss. Arise from your slumbers, and let young and old, endeavor to do all in their power to accomplish the desired object, and you soon will be fully rewarded, and you will speak with pride of your efforts, and success. But enough, we know too well that this momentary indifference will soon be substituted by energetic and zealous action, and that at our next visit to the beautiful city of Monroe, we will behold the fruits of their labor by hearing a good sermon

---

[30]The three holidays to which Wessolowsky refers are the two days of *Rosh Hashanah* (pronounced Rosh-ha-show-nah), the Jewish New Year, and *Yom Kippur* (pronounced Yom-key-poor), the Day of Atonement.

delivered by some Rabbi, and the children advanced in the Mosaic teachings.[31]

Otherwise, our brethren here are enjoying a very enviable reputation, some of them being town officers, and having the confidence of our Gentile friends.

In their business, they are very prosperous, and all seem to do well.

The B. B. Lodge, though very young, is performing its noble mission, and seems to be in a very prosperous condition. We lectured in the temple publicly, and in the B. B. Lodge.

We met Mr. George Stein, an accomplished and scholarly gentleman, who resided heretofore in Eufaula, Ala., and who has treated us very kindly. To Mr. Kuhn, the *South* is thankful for service rendered.

We have nothing special to mention of Monroe except that we were highly flattered and honored by the complimentary letter received of Mr. John H. Dinkgrave, an attorney-at-law, at Monroe, speaking of the esteem of ourselves, and truthfulness of all facts stated in our lecture, and although a Gentile, he was glad that it had been stated, and would be delighted if such a record could be given of the "American Citizen."

We spent several days in Monroe, and were indeed pleased to have met our brothers there. We departed for Farmersville, and arrived there Saturday evening, a distance of thirty-five miles from Monroe, which we had to travel in a stage, over a most fearful and hilly road. It seemed to us that roads in Louisiana are very much neglected.

It is a disgrace to a civilized country that roads are not kept in better order, and thus lessen the danger and risk of travel; it is undoubtedly a criminal negligence and ought to be looked after by the proper authorities. We took courage sometimes, walking over a dangerous bridge or a bad piece of road, and at last succeeded to reach our place for destination, Farmersville, Saturday night, where we were received by Mr. Stein and family in a princely style, and we freely enjoyed the hospitality of that good mother in Israel.

---

[31]According to tradition Moses was the "great teacher." He not only accepted God's covenant for the people of Israel. At the same time, he received a host of ritual, religious, and moral injunctions the recitation of which was committed to writing as "The Book of Torah."

But here we must stop; will give you outlines of Farmersville, Bastrop and Vicksburg next.

We regret that our letter giving details of Baton Rouge, La., did not reach you. It contained a full description of the old capital and of everything that would have been interesting.

Alas! It is not our fault. We wish we had His Fraudulency, R. B. Hayes, by the ears for appointing officers who are foolish and silly enough to pocket a letter because it is a *weightier* one than usual, even without money. But why blame Hayes? Is he not conforming strictly to the civil service reform? Has he not shown it very plainly in the case of the Hon. Simon Wolf?[32] We await your answer.

W.

---

[32]Simon Wolf (1836-1923) was a German-born lawyer and lobbyist. During the Civil War he was a lawyer in Washington and after the 1868 election defended Ulysses S. Grant against charges of anti-Semitism. In return, he was awarded the post of recorder of deeds in the District of Columbia. He held that post until 1877 when political pressures associated with scandals of corruption forced his resignation. After a term as a judge in the District of Columbia and a two year tour as American consul to Egypt, in 1882, he returned to private law practice and became a spokesman for the Jewish community.

Letter Number Five

Charles Wessolowsky to Rabbi Edward B. M. Browne

Greenville, Mississippi
June 1878

• • •

[*Wessolowsky praises the activities of the B'nai B'rith Lodge and Ladies Benevolent Society in Farmersville, Louisiana; in Bastrop, Louisiana, he mentions the purchase of a Methodist Church for a synagogue by the Jewish community which he feels will round out the community and complement the presence of an active B'nai B'rith Lodge and a Ladies Hebrew Benevolent Society; in Vicksburg, Mississippi, he describes his quarters at the Washington Hotel; talks of Dr. Gotthelf, the Rabbi of the Vicksburg Jewish congregation who is also on the city's Board of Education; relates that the Vicksburg congregation boasts of several Jewish social and charitable lodges; and applauds the community's civic, economic and social activities.*]

• • •

Farmersville is a small city, situated in the northern part of Louisiana, about eighteen miles from the Arkansas line, numbers about six hundred inhabitants, among whom there are about sixteen Jewish families, and in all about one hundred Jewish souls.

There is a B'nai B'rith Lodge, lately instituted, and seems to be in a very flourishing condition. Our brothers here as elsewhere, are engaged in the mercantile pursuits, and D. Stein & Co. is doing the largest and most extensive business in this part of the country. H. Brown, and others, are also doing a good business.

We had an invitation to attend their regular Lodge meeting, in which elections took place, and brother L. J. Levy was elected President; although a young brother, yet he is fully enwrapped in the cause of B. B., and we feel confident that Farmersville Lodge will prosper under his guidance, particularly being aided by brothers Stein, the Monitor, and Brown, the out-going President, and other brothers who are desirous and working energetically to make their Lodge, although in a remote corner, second to none.

Here, also the noble mothers, in Israel, have done their share of duty, have had for the past years a "Ladies Benevolent Society," which had dispensed a great deal of charity, but is now dissolved, turning over all funds on hand to the B'nai B'rith Lodge (and of which the *Jewish South* has taken notice, publishing the resolution to that effect). Mrs. Stein, who is known as a charitable and benevolent lady, had aided and assisted in bringing about the success of the ladies' society, and she with the other Jewish ladies undoubtedly deserve the respect and honor of all Israelites; and would it be well for others in other small places to follow their example? Thus we remained here for a few days, and our stay was made very pleasant by all our brethren, particularly by the treatment received at the hands of our hosts, the Stein family. We are indebted to brother N. Lehman for courtesies, and we wish that we may be enabled to reciprocate the kindness shown towards us.

Tuesday morning we left for Bastrop (a distance of about thirty miles) by buggy, another small city in the same part of Louisiana, and we were pleased to see the roads in that part of the country in much better and safer condition, and after crossing many bayous by flat, and passing through Ouachita, where we met our brother Wolf of the firm of Wolf & Wise, and who received us very kindly, we arrived at our place of destination in the evening, and were soon conducted to the elegant residence of brother Wolf, of the firm of Wolf & Silvernagel. Here we found the Yehudim [Hebrews] all well to do; they number about twenty families, and are indeed deserving a special mention. Determined to promote the cause of Judaism and to elevate themselves in the eyes of the Gentiles, they have lately purchased a Methodist church, which they will remodel into a Synagogue, or build a new one and are on the lookout to obtain the services of a Rabbi who is capable to teach Hebrew and English,[33] and are willing to give their might towards paying liberally the one

---

[33]The German Jews, like other immigrant minorities, while having to deal with the demands of learning new languages, preferred the comfort of their own tongue and the company of their countrymen. One of the requirements laid down by many congregations for prospective religious leaders was the capacity to help in the transformation by teaching English for acculturating purposes and Hebrew for religious reasons. This was particularly true for reform-leaning congregations which did not wish to have the entire liturgy in Hebrew but wished to replace the portions read in the German vernacular with English.

who can occupy and fill the position in all its branches. Here, also, the banner of B'nai B'rith has been planted, and a prosperous and good working Lodge is in existence. We were invited to address them, which we cheerfully accepted, and also gave a public lecture Wednesday night.

A Ladies Hebrew Benevolent Society, of which Mrs. Silvernagel is President, Mrs. Levy, Vice-President, Mrs. Symon, Secretary, and Mrs. Heller, Treasurer, is performing its charitable function to a great extent and many poor Israelites who, I understand, are of late frequent visitors at Bastrop, have received their due aid and their wants alleviated by the purse of those noble women. We were also glad to see that some of our brethren here and in Farmersville are holding public offices, and are giving satisfaction to all. Through the courtesies of some of our brothers, who were appointed by the Lodge as a special committee to solicit subscriptions, the *Jewish South*, has received its full share of patronage from Jew and Gentile, for which we express our grateful acknowledgements.

Thursday morning we bade adieu to Bastrop, whose inhabitants we will ever remember. A buggy conveyed us again to Monroe, about twenty-eight miles distant; we remained there only one day owing to our indisposition, stopping with our friend Kaliski; the following day we started for Vicksburg, where we arrived about noon, and made Washington Hotel our headquarters.

This hotel bears the proper name, as it resembles in grandeur, comfort and particularly in "bill of fare," the hotels fair in the revolutionary times of Washington—it stands proudly in the midst of Vicksburg, like Washington, "the father of our country," as the father of hotels, representing aged antiquity, and boastingly defying all modern improvements. The gas is substituted by coal oil, the rooms large enough for our Jewish ladies to fatten their geese for Pesach [Passover]; the furniture therein of the style of the chair and table used by Washington, which are on exhibition in Independence Hall at Philadelphia, and the *fare* very *unfair* for the charges made; but thanks to the courtesies of our friends, we found other channels to satisfy our palate, and which indeed were very acceptable. In this, Mrs. Hornthal was very instrumental, having spent at her house all day Sunday, enjoying her hospitalities so lavishly bestowed and the company of the interesting family, of which the charming and accomplished Miss B. is a member, and whose efforts in behalf of making our visit pleasant and agreeable, we appreciate very much, having been invited there by that refined gentleman, Mr. Moses Lovenstein, whose fortune it is to be an inmate of that family, and to enjoy constantly the pleasure and comforts of such a *home.* Sunday morning we were invited to attend and to address a B'nai B'rith meeting of Vicksburg Lodge to which also the members of Enrogel Lodge were invited. We spoke upon the works of the order. Vicksburg Lodge is fitting up a beautiful hall with all modern improvements, for their place of meeting. Enrogel Lodge also is industriously working for the promotion of the cause.

There is also here a Lodge of the Free Sons,[34] of which brother Kuhn is President, and a Kesher Lodge,[35] brother L. Hirsh is President.

The congregation Anshe Chesed,[36] with Mr. Brown as President, and Rev. Dr. Gotthelf as their spiritual guide, seems to flourish, although an addition to the roll of membership would indeed be very gratifying to the cause of Judaism.

Dr. Gotthelf, whose labor, zeal and love for the cause of Judaism, within the past thirty-five years as minister in Louisville and Vicksburg, is so widely known and appreciated that I indeed feel at a loss what to say of him, save that although having reached the age of sixty, he is yet vigorous and strong, working industriously in the pulpit and otherwise to elevate and glorify Judaism, and well may the Israelites of Vicksburg be proud of having as their spiritual guide one, who is ever open and candid in his expressions, and to

---

[34]The Free Sons of Israel, or I. F. S. of I., is a Jewish fraternal order founded in 1849 in New York. Its initial purpose was to end the prohibition against Jewish expropriation.

[35]Kesher Lodge refers to a local lodge of Order Kesher Shel Barzel, or K. S. B. Along with the Free Sons of Israel and B'nai B'rith, it was one of the four major Jewish fraternal orders of the 19th century. It was dedicated to education, support and care for widows and orphans and the aged, as well as with distributing charity. Like its fellow-Jewish fraternal orders, it reflected a growing tendency in the United States of forming non-synagogue organizations to carry out philanthropic responsibilites.

[36]*Anshe Chesed* (pronounced an-sha che-said with a gutteral -ch) means "People of Loving Kindness."

expound that what he believes to be right and just, and who is so much liked by our Gentile friend. He was lately elected a member of the School Board, defeating a very popular Gentile. I hope that he will be spared for many more years, and that, he, by his known ability and eloquence in the pulpit, will continue to expound the true doctrine and teachings of Judaism.

Last but not least, our Jewish ladies here also have their society, a Ladies' Hebrew Benevolent Association, of which the popular Mrs. Hornthal has been President for seven years, and now positively declining to accept a re-election, Mrs. Kuhn was chosen in her place.

Monday night we lectured in the Temple as per announcement and had a very fair audience. The evening paper requested us to repeat the lecture, but could not comply for want of time.

Through the kindness of Mr. Lovenstein we enjoyed a ride out to the famous National Cemetery, in company with Mrs. Hornthal and Dr. Gotthelf. Human skill, art and labor have so beautified and adorned and so gorgeously arranged the place that we thought it more fitting to be the Park of Vicksburg than a graveyard. Sixteen thousand soldiers are said to be buried here, of whom three thousand only are known, thirteen thousand unknown. A marble slab, rounded on the top, with the number of each grave on it adorns each grave, and is there to show the appreciation of a government for its defenders. The beautiful rides all around it, the splendid roads fitted up for the purpose, the constant labor employed in trimming the hedges and to keep even the growing grass, all aids and adds to its beauty. Thousands are spent here to beautify a place, to make it an *Eden*, while perhaps the orphans of some who are sleeping there are in want of raiment and food to be protected from the cold and hunger. In a little brick building is a show-case, containing different trinkets found upon the dead bodies and on their clothes, some known and others unknown. Nothing of value or interest is in it, save a few rings, old watches, etc. We entered our name upon the register and returned to Vicksburg.

Thus we enjoyed a splended drive, and had the opportunity of seeing Vicksburg and then returned to the home of our friend, where an elegant repast was spread before us, of which we partook heartily. After supper, we met many young ladies and gentlemen, and were pleased to form their acquaintance.

The Israelites here number about one hundred families; as usual, they have the sway of the business and are well off. There is not one retail dry goods carried on by a Gentile.

We made the acquaintance of many, but desire to give special mention of Messrs. G. Fisher and L. Hirsch, who so courteously and kindly rendered valuable service to the *Jewish South*.

We also met Mr. Lovenberg, the popular Justice of the Peace, and the great artist in performing surgical operations; also, Mr. Max Sokolosky, who I learn has been a second Frankland in the epidemic at Vicksburg,[37] risking his own life in administering to the wants of the sufferers, nursing the sick and burying the dead, and doing all within his power, day and night to aid and assist all those who were needy. All honor to brother Sokoloski. We were proud to see that medal, with the suitable inscription, given to him by Vicksburg Lodge as in appreciation of his services. May he ever wear it with pride and honor to himself and humanity at large.

The Jewish temple here is handsome and neatly fitted up inside, but it is very much in want of improvement on external appearance. We learn that our brethren intend to give it a brushing sometime this winter, and the money is to be raised by the energetic and talented young men and ladies of Vicksburg, who will give exhibitions of various kinds.

The wide-awake and go-ahead firm of Waggenstein & Heman have lately fitted up in the centre of the business of the city, a beautiful garden, called the "Southern Garden," for the accommodation of their visitors who desire to indulge in a glass of

---

[37]The "Frankland" Wessolowsky refers to here is mentioned again in letter number six as the "hero of Memphis." Apparently this Frankland had performed outstanding service during the epidemic referred to here and later in letter number eight. This yellow fever (or "yellow jack," as Wessolowsky calls it in letter eight) was similar to the one which ravaged the South in 1872. The epidemic raced down the Mississippi from Memphis to the Delta. The entire Jewish population in the South geared up to deal with this scourge. *The Jewish South* established a Yellow Fever Fund, and all of the fraternal, social, and charitable organizations throughout the South collected monies, food, and clothing, while the membership cared for the sick and assumed the responsibility of caring for the widowed and orphaned. The fraternal organizations, B'nai B'rith in particular, even mobilized the resources of its member lodges outside the South. Apparently this particular "yellow jack" epidemic raged during the months of August and September in 1878.

beer or a good square meal, in a place which is airy, clean and nicely fitted up for the comfort of ladies and gentlemen. As an appetizer, they furnish you fragrance of flowers, and sweet music every night by a celebrated string band, and sometimes they procure the services of some nightingale, who treats the audience with her thrilling and sweet vocal music.

Thursday noon, we were reminded that the boat going up the river is about ready to start, and we soon found ourself on the "Maud,"steaming up the "Father of the Waters" for Greenville. We arrived there Friday morning, and became the guest of the great friends to our Chief, Mr. and Mrs. Pohl.

Apropos, we must not forget to mention that those old stand-bys, "Hank Rosenbaum and Dave Cromeline," were with us in the city of Vicksburg and contributed much in making our stay a pleasant one.

W.

Letter Number Six

Charles Wessolowsky to Rabbi Edward B. M. Browne

Atlanta, Georgia
July 1878

• • •

[*Wessolowsky mentions fifty families in Greenville, Mississippi, that compose the Jewish community with two B'nai B'rith Lodges and a Young Men's Hebrew Benevolent Society; next stop is Pine Bluff, Arkansas, in which he states that all the Jewish social and charitable orders are represented and active under the guidance of a Rabbi; Little Rock, Arkansas, is last stop on this tour; Here the Jewish community has a "Hebrew Children's Mite Society,"allowing Jewish children to engage in charitable acts; briefly sketches Jewish religious, social and economic life in Memphis, Tennessee; and returns to Georgia.*]

• • •

All in all Greenville, Miss., is a pretty little city of thirty-five hundred inhabitants, among whom are about five hundred Jewish souls, including about fifty Jewish families. Although we were not feeling well, yet our host and hostess have made our stay pleasant, and doing all in their power not to let us miss our home in time of sickness. We have made several acquaintances; met Messrs. Marshall and Morris, whose acquintances we had formed in the Grand Lodge at New Orleans, and we were treated by all most courteously. Special mention we must make of the acquaintance of the most obliging and accommodating Postmaster, Mr. Jake Alexander, and Mr. Marx Gunzberger. Both these gentlemen, together with our host, Mr. Pohl, have placed us under obligations for their generous treatment, and we shall forever remember them kindly.

There are here two B'nai B'rith Lodges, and both seem to flourish well. We lectured in Greenville Lodge Sunday morning, to which Amity Lodge was invited, and most of its members were present to hear us. We trust that the initiatory step taken by these Lodges to visit one another will be continued and that both will mutually work in behalf of the good and the advancement of the order in peace and harmony.[38]

Monday night, we gave a public lecture at the Opera House to a large audience, which was received very favorably; and Tuesday, though not feeling well at all, we lectured at the Masonic Hall, upon invitation extended to us by the Young Men's Hebrew Benevolent Society [Y.M.H.B.S.]. This society deserves great credit and is worthy of notice. It was started by about fifteen young men, who have felt the necessity of the formation of a society which will aid and alleviate the wants of unfortunate young men who cannot obtain work, although very willing to earn their livelihood, and who, as a class, are generally neglected by our philanthropists, for reasons that they are "young and can't work." These young men of the Society bestow charity upon all who call on them, yet their chief aim is to assist those unfortunate young men, and as we learned, they already have done a great deal, and many young men to-day owe their present comfortable situation to that Y.M.H.B.S., who provided for their wants and comfort while in Greenville, and from there sent them to other places. This Y.M. Society was the only one in existence in the South as far as we have ascertained, until recently, when the leading Jewish young men of New Orleans started one similar and are also performing their missions nobly.

Through the courtesy of Messrs. Wise and Goldstein, we enjoyed a ride through the city, and admired the beautiful cottages owned by our co-religionists and the various handsome churches which adorned the city. Would to heaven that I could chronicle the existence of a Jewish temple, which would be of a vast benefit to our Jewish brethren in Greenville, and in particular to the rising generation. These youths, are receiving their instructions at the

---

[38]Obviously, there are indications such as this entry in Wessolowsky's letters that the all-important function for B'nai B'rith to serve as a unifying bond among Jewry was not always sufficiently strong enough to overcome stronger emotional cultural differences and liturgical disagreements. Consequently, even small towns such as Greenville could have more than one B'nai B'rith lodge, a reflection of the friction and division within the Jewish community. In the larger cities each large congregation had a B. B. lodge of its own, or several congregations joined together for the purpose of forming a B. B. Lodge. The existence of several lodges in such cities as St. Louis did not necessarily indicate division as it did the limits of size, distance and a propensity to be with one's "own kind."

hands of Mr. Rawitzer, who is an accomplished teacher, yet the teaching in a temple has a greater impression and remains more deeply engraved in the heart of a child than elsewhere; and Greenville is fortunate enough to boast of many young ones.

We enjoyed the hospitalities of Mrs. Alexander, Mrs. Gunzberg, Mrs. Goldstein and Mrs. Wise, the latter giving us a splendid banquet to a great many friends Monday night after the lecture. We met Mrs. Landauer, the daughter of our friend, Mrs. Michael, of Waterloo, La., at whose house we enjoyed an elegant entertainment, given by the Y.M.H.B. Society after our lecture Tuesday night. Thus we were most princely treated in Greenville, and though sick, enjoyed the hospitalities lavished upon us so bountifully until Wednesday morning, and after bidding adieu to all, we departed for Pine Bluff, up the Mississippi to Arkansas City, where we remained all night, and took the train in the morning, which landed us safely at Pine Bluff in the evening, and where we were most cordially received by that prince of princes, Mr. Sam Franklin and his lady.

Apropos, I will not omit to mention that in Greenville you can find another individual to be added to the list of the Jewish Cabinet for Mrs. Hayes—our mutual friend, Mr. Pohl, who is City Treasurer, has succeeded within twelve months to bring the city out of debt, which is now in very easy circumstances. Would like to call the attention of Mr. Hayes to the above, and perhaps he will condescend to appoint some Jew to some prominent office.[39]

Here in Pine Bluff we have met a great many friends and admirers of our Chief, who are anxious to meet him again. Our co-religionists, who are mostly engaged in mercantile pursuits, are

---

[39]This is a curious statement since in 1879 William Evarts, Secretary of State under Hayes, stated that "this government has ever felt a deep interest in the welfare of the Hebrew race in foreign countries." Evarts had sent a directive to John Kasson, American Minister in Vienna, who was conducting negotiations for establishing official relations between the United States and Rumania. His statement was issued to directly instruct Kasson to comment on the Rumanian government's persecution of its Jewish communities in spite of the requirement laid down by article 44 of the Treaty of Berlin (by which Rumania secured her independence from Turkey in 1878) which required Rumania to grant complete civil and political rights to all her citizens. See Rufus Learsi, *The Jews in America* (New York: World, 1954).

doing well, and some of our brethren are pursuing agriculture to a very large extent. Thus, Mr. Gabe Meyer, the President of the congregation, owns nineteen plantations, all of which are cultivated very successfully; and Mr. Sol Franklin, brother of our host, has about nineteen hundred acres in cotton, from which he expected to realized a handsome profit.

It was our own good fortune to meet here that famous personage, Dr. Lisinsky, who is a perfect prodigy. The greatest singer, the most eloquent orator, a graceful dancer, in short, he is all perfection. Pine Bluff would be a dull place without Dr. Lisinsky. The Doctor prides himself not a little on the beautiful goldheaded cane presented him by his pupils on the Sabbath-school.

Nearly every Jewish order has planted its standard here, and all Lodges seem to be in a flourishing condition. The B'nai B'rith Lodge, with brother Morris Altschule as President, will no doubt succeed well, and we were pleased to see that another Lodge will soon be started there, (all obstacles having been removed) which will give an opportunity to a great many outsiders to join the order.

There is also here a lodge of Kesher Shel Barsel [K. S. B.], with A. Meyer as President, one of the Free Sons of Israel, with brother J. Berlin as President. I was told that these lodges all are acting harmoniously, and all doing their full share of duty.

There are two Ladies' Relief Societies—The Ladies' Aid Society—President, Mrs. E. Miller; and the Ladies' Relief Society—President, Mrs. Rosenberg—both of which are dispensing their charities in the fullest measure to all who are in need and worthy of the same.

The Congregation, "Anshe Emeth,"[40] with G. Meyer as President, and Rev. Mr. Greenblatt as their spiritual guide, seems to be in very healthy circumstances, and we regret very much that we did not find the reverend gentleman at home, and were deprived of his acquaintance. They have a fine temple and an excellent choir.

The affable brother, Mr. Mehlinger, placed us under obligation, with his pleasing disposition, his willingness and readiness to work in our behalf.

We remained in Pine Bluff nearly four days and were most

---

[40]*Anshe Emeth* (pronounched an-sha eh-meth) means "People of Truth."

happy to meet the friend of our Chief, Miss R. B., in whose house we spent a delightful evening.

Tuesday evening we left for Little Rock, and landed there safely Wednesday evening.

This city made a very favorable impression upon us, and after a sojourn of five days, our "first impressions" of the place have been confirmed and materially strengthened. There are some fine and imposing buildings in the business portion of the city, and the residences are very pretty. Through courtesies extended us by Mrs. Leon Pollock, we enjoyed a ride through the city, and had an opportunity to observe the ornamental floral display in the front yard of almost every residence, which is indeed charming and beautiful.

Our co-religionists, who are thrifty and good merchants, are in a prosperous condition. Intelligence and respectability will compare here favorably with that of almost any city, and we were proud to know that we were deceived in our ideas that the people of Arkansas are ruffianly and uncivilized. Civility, refinement and culture exist here in its highest standard, and the early history of such characters as the famous "Arkansas Traveler," has long since become a myth.

We were most hospitably treated by our co-religionists, and we are under many obligations to Messrs. L. Ehrenberg, Phil. Pfeiffer and A. Pollock for courtesies shown us during our stay in Little Rock.

Those three gentlemen, together with others, tendered us an invitation to lecture, which we accepted, and did lecture in their handsomely fitted-up temple to a very fair and intelligent audience. A public reception was also given to us at Dwell's Park, an elegant place for pleasure seekers, where we were honored with resolutions of acknowledgement and appreciation by that scholarly gentleman, Mr. L. Ehrenberg, in a neat and appropriate speech, which has taken us by a great surprise, not being aware of the proceedings. There we met all the Jewish ladies and gentlemen, among whom I must not fail to mention the venerable lady, the mother of our townsman, Mr. Charles Pfeiffer, who, although aged is vigorous, and seems to be in splendid health. We met also Mr. and Mrs. A. Block, whom we knew in Georgia, and whom we were very glad to see.

The Congregation B'nai Israel,[41] President Simon Gans, is in a very flourishing condition, and the officiating rabbi, Mr. Block, is very much liked and appreciated. We were proud at forming his acquaintance and that of his interesting family, and hope that we will meet again.

There is also here a B. B. Lodge, President A. Kemper, and a K. S. B.,L. Loeb as President, all seems to prosper.

Our Jewish ladies here are doing their duty and have a Ladies Hebrew Benevolent Society, President, Mrs. A. Ottenheimer. But we found here another society of which we as an Israelite are very proud, and which is worthy of example to other places. A society formed by Hebrew children, styling themselves "Hebrew Children's Mite Society," for the purpose of aiding the New Orleans Orphans Home. Its officers are Leon Louis, President, Morris Wellman, V.P.; Louis Pollack, Secretary, and Otto Ottenheimer, Treasurer. This society gives various entertainments and realizes a nice sum of money, which is forwarded to the Orphans Home at New Orleans. Is this not noble, generous and praiseworthy? We are proud of you, children of Israel, and we hope that you will continue, and grow up to be good and useful men and women.

Our stay at Little Rock, has been made by all very pleasant and very agreeable, and we cannot fail to mention that we enjoyed the entertainment at the residence of Mrs. M. Katsenstein, on the night of our departure, where we had the pleasure of meeting a large number of beautiful ladies, and we are thankful to them for the teaching we received in the art of *Klopher*,[42] and we hope that when we have the honor of meeting them again that they will initiate us, and give us the full degrees.

We left Little Rock for Hot Springs, where we remained several days; met many acquaintances, observed the beauties and curiosities of nature, and left fully satisfied, *with what we have seen* at Hot Springs. We returned to Little Rock, where we again

---

[41] *B'nai Israel* means "Sons of Israel."

[42] The *Klopher* was a German dance often utilizing wooden shoes to make a knocking or "klophering" sound much as taps on tap shoes. This knocking of the shoes on the floor was accompanied by the hand-slapping of knees and bottom of the shoes as well as snapping of the fingers and clapping of the hands. (Compare "clogging.")

remained Friday and then departed for Memphis on the Memphis and Little Rock Railroad, which, by the way, is in a splendid condition and affords every comfort to the traveling public, and arrived at our place of destination Thursday morning and soon found ourselves in that elegant hotel, the Gaston House, where we enjoyed all the luxuries and comforts a modern hotel can offer.

Here we met Mr. Gunzberger, the brother of our worthy friend of Greenville, Miss., also Mr. Frankland, the "hero of Memphis," Mr. Selig, the ex-G. P. of D. G. L. No. 7,[43] and Mr. H. Bijah, who has shown us a great many courtesies, and to whom we are indebted for many pleasures enjoyed while in Memphis.

We attended Friday night services at the temple,[44] where Mr. Frankland officiated in the absence of Rev. Mr. Samfield, and had the pleasure of forming the acquaintance of the great scholar and gentleman, Rev. Mr. F. Sarner, the rabbi of the other congregation.

Upon request, we lectured Sunday morning in the beautiful Lodge-room of the Symon Tuska Lodge, and Monday, having received a dispatch to return home at once in order to fill the editorial chair of our Chief during his absence at the Congress of Stockholm,[45] we left Memphis and arrived in Atlanta Tuesday night, were received by the entire staff and employees, and felt that we were once more upon Georgia soil.

Thus our most pleasant trip through the Southwest ended, and here we will take occasion again to return our hearty and sincere thanks to all our friends, and to all who so kindly and hospitably extended their civilities and courtesies to us during our stay with

---

[43]These initials stand for Grand President of District Grand Lodge No. 7.

[44]Using the ancient calendar by which days were designated with the rising and setting of the Sun, the Jewish Sabbath begins at sundown Friday and lasts until sundown on Saturday, rather than from midnight to midnight. The Sabbath is heralded in by the wife's lighting of the Sabbath candles on Friday at sundown. The joy of the Sabbath is reflected in the singing of a 16th century poem written by Moses Cordovers of Safed entitled *Lecha Dodi* (pronounced Leh-haw doe-dee) which means "come, my friend, to meet the bride," that is, the Sabbath was "last" in the order or creation, but "first" in thought. The Sabbath is joyous rest from the pettiness of the everyday world and rest in communion with God—and thus is the pinnacle of the creative purpose.

[45]This was one of the many conventions attended by Browne that strove to promote interfaith brotherhood.

them; and to our friends in Bayou Sara and Baton Rouge, Louisiana, we desire to say, that we hope when we see them again, that they will have forgiven those careless post office officials who have lost our letter, giving the sketches of their respective cities.

W.

Letter Number Seven

Charles Wessolowsky to Rabbi Edward B. M. Browne

New Orleans, Louisiana
March 1879

• • •

[*A brief stop in Montgomery, Alabama, on the way to New Orleans allows for little more than a mentioning of a few names and a comment on the high position held by Jews in Montgomery civic and economic circles; Wessolowsky speaks of the Selma, Alabama, Jewish community remodeling its temple; in Meridian, Mississippi, he praises the newly constructed temple that was financed by the energies of twenty families; Next, in Mobile, Alabama, he discusses the performance of Dr. Moses, Rabbi of the Jewish community.*]

• • •

Again we are on the wings and willing to give a birds-eye view over the cities, towns, hamlets and other places, where we can greet and meet our friends, brothers and acquaintances—and when we reached Montgomery, we thought A-la-ba-ma, "here we rest"—

We met our genial friend and gentlemanly orator, Bro. Emile Jacobi, the past president of the D. G. L. No. 7, who although very busy, has shown us a great deal of attention, and our old friend Joe H. with his usual happy smile was pleased to see us. We had a hearty hand-shaking. We had the acquaintance of Rev. H. Hecht, the minister of the Hebrew Congregation of Montgomery, whom we find to be a gentleman of learning and refinement. Our stay was very brief and we regret exceedingly, that we could not attend the wedding of Miss Nannette Weil to Mr. Alex Rice, as pressing business in New Orleans forced us to leave Montgomery the evening of the 26th instead, and we take occasion now to return our thanks to Mr. Weil for invitation, and wish the couple a safe voyage upon the matrimonial sea.

Brevity of time deprived us of receiving the necessary information of all Jewish matters in Montgomery, and we are forced to forgo the pleasure of giving a detailed statement of the same. Suffice to say that our co-religionists in Montgomery are held in high estimation by their Christian brethren and even the mayor of the city is an Israelite, the Hon. Mordecai Moses, who with his zeal and energy works for the welfare of the city, and his ability as a financier has succeeded in establishing the credit of the city equally as good as that of any other in the Union.

The evening train brought us to Selma, where we remained over night under the roof of our friends Mr. and Mrs. Schuster and were glad to find them in good health, full of anticipated joy and anxiously awaiting the occasion of their silver wedding, to which they invited their friends and acquaintances from several adjoining States. Mr. and Mrs. Schuster will please accept our best wishes and we assure them, that if we live, to make good our promise and be presented at the celebration of their golden wedding.

Our friend Kayser is still at his post, full of life and good jokes, and ever ready to serve his friends. If in our power, we would like to vote for him as Kaiser (mayor) of Selma. But who can tell what the future may bring forth? Men who are not *Kayser* have made *Kaiser*, then, why should he, who has the full claim, title and right to *Kayser* not be made *Kaiser*, at least of the Empire of Selma? We feel that the voters of Selma will think as we do and elevate this useful witty gentleman, though small, to the high position of Honorable Mayor of Selma.

We were glad to hear that our co-religionists in Selma have given a fair and realized about three thousand dollars which amount they are applying to the remodeling of their Synagogue—the work is progressing rapidly; when finished, it promises to be a handsome edifice, which will bestow credit and honor upon them.

In the morning we departed for Meridian, Mississippi, where we landed in due time, and were greeted by the shout of hotel drummers, soliciting customers for their respective hotels. Being an entire stranger in the city and not knowing what hotel to make our headquarters, we followed one who brought us to the European House, F. Weitman, proprietor, and indeed we were pleased with our accidental solicitor. This House though but lately opened, has a proprietor, who is an old hotel keeper. For the benefit of the traveling public I will state, that the gentleman is thoroughly versed in his line of business, and that in his House they will find all the comforts and good attention which hotels can offer, and that his table is supplied by the markets of Mobile and New Orleans, and in all is kept in first class style.

In the morning we ventured out and soon found Mr. Lesser, a gentleman whom we met at the Grand Lodge in New Orleans. We were both pleased to meet again, soon was I made to feel by him that, although a stranger in Meridian yet among brothers. I met Rev. Mr. Weinstein the *chazen* and minister of the congregation, who exhibiting his usual courtesy and politeness introduced me to all our brothers, and was requested by the President and Vice-President, and the Reverend to lecture that evening—being Friday night in the Temple, and to our greatest astonishment and delightful surprise, we beheld a magnificent structure, a gorgeous temple, which indeed in beauty, neatness and elegance equals to many that we have seen in larger cities. It is the only building in the city which is lighted by gas (manufactured in the rear of the temple) and which adds a great deal to the attraction of the building. This noble work, the accomplishment of this grand deed is well worthy to be held up as a pattern to many of our co-religionists in Georgia and elsewhere;[46] only twenty-two Jewish families, and in all perhaps about one hundred and fifty souls, have by determination, adequate will and energetic works, erected a structure which today stands with its majestic towers, in grandeur and splendor, as an honor to our people and a pride to the citizens of Meridian. Indeed here we are made to feel and understand the meaning of the Prophet *"a few will become a mighty nation"* and here we have seen it clearly demonstrated, that Judaism is not dead, that it seeks its elevation and advancement at all places, where the sons of the dispersed nation have planted themselves. All honor to our co-religionists in Meridian, and we say to them, "well done thou true and faithful servants."

According to promise we delivered a short lecture in the temple Friday night, and soon thereafter were requested to deliver a public lecture on Sunday night, which (thinking that we could spend Sunday as pleasantly in Meridian as elsewhere) we accepted. In the morning we visited the Sunday School, superintended by Rev. Weinstein, and assisted by two other young gentlemen, whose names we do not now remember, addressed the children and found

---

[46]*Jewish South*, 17 March 1879.

them proficient in the Biblical history, catechism, etc.[47] In the evening we lectured upon invitation to the B. B. Lodge, and at night again in the temple, to a large audience of Jews and Gentiles.

The congregation is officered as follows: J. Marks, President, D. Rosenbaum, Vice-President, Mr. S. Weinstein, Minister,—is in splendid condition, and Asaph Lodge No. 286, I. O. B. B. with S. Wenner as President is progressing fairly.

Here also we found our Jewish ladies enlisted in the noble work of aiding and assisting in all that is kind and generous, and they gave a Purim Ball[48] for the purpose of raising funds, to more beautify their handsome edifice. I hope that like *Esther*[49] of old, success has crowned their undertakings and that no *Haman*[50] has crossed their path.

---

[47]The Sunday School had its roots in the economic necessity of keeping shop open on the Sabbath, the busiest day of the week when a store did approximately 75-80% of its business, and the need to acculturate the outward trappings of the educational process utilized by the Jewish community to the model set by the surrounding Christian churches. Wessolowsky's use of the term, *catechism*, a distinctly Catholic institution, is curious. A catechism is absent in Judaism because of the absence of a central authority in determining belief. He may be using the term in its broader meaning of memorization and the question-and-answer method of instruction.

[48]*Purim* (pronounced poor-im) literally means "lots." It commemorates a day on which the Jews were saved from their oppressors. Read on the evening and morning of the holiday, the book of Esther records the deliverance of the Jews during their period of captivity in Persia. It is a holiday that is celebrated with great merriment including the eating of a cake called *Hamantaschen*, "ears of Haman," named after the chief courtier of the king who would have killed all the Jews. Among the finest of the *Purim* practices is the sending of gifts of food to friends, and money to the poor. Among the traditional means of celebrating the event are *Purim* parties and balls.

[49]Esther was the Jewish wife of King Ahasuerus who, upon the pleading of her father Mordecai, went to the king at the danger of her own life to uncover the devious plot of his chief adviser.

[50]Haman was the chief adviser against whom Esther successfully spoke and whose punishment for plotting against Esther's people and for attempting to dupe the king was death. During the recitation of the Book of Esther on *Purim*, noise-makers are handed out and, according to tradition, every time Haman's name is mentioned, the congregation makes noise and stamps feet to drown out the mere utterance of his name as another gesture of deliverance and joy, and of contempt for what he represents.

To these ladies and gentlemen that have bestowed upon us courtesies and attentions, we return our thanks, and assure them that our visit at Meridian will ever be remembered by us.

Monday we took the train for Mobile, and arrived there safely, stopping with our old friend Mr. J. Loventhal, who spared nothing to make our stay in Mobile pleasant and agreeable. We were highly pleased to meet again the learned and cultured Dr. Moses, in whose house we spent Saturday and were delightfully entertained by his interesting family and relations. We heard the Doctor discourse in German, Saturday morning, and we were indeed delighted with it. It recalled to us the days of yore when we heard preaching in German language by our celebrated men in Germany.[51] The Doctor gives a shape of the history and teachings of old, what effect they have upon us now, the simplicity and plainness, of Esther when she approached her King and Lord. It was an excellent sermon and our co-religionists in Mobile may be proud of their Minister who is not less learned in the English language, and in which he preaches every alternate Saturday.[52]

We are pleased to see that the Israelites of Mobile are appreciating the work of their Minister and a large number of them attended divine worship every Friday evening and Saturday morning.

The Choir in Mobile as well as in Meridian is very fine, reflects credit upon them and their leader.

After bidding adieu to our numerous friends and acquaintances in Mobile, we left Sunday for New Orleans, and that night brought

---

[51]Obviously, though the Jewish presence in Mobile dated back to the 18th century and its congregation was founded in 1842, there must have been a sufficient flow of new German-born immigrants into Mobile for the next 35 years to require the use of German in the service.

[52]Saturday, until sundown, is the Jewish Sabbath on which day, during the religious services, a portion of the Torah is read, and during which day all work is supposed to cease. The celebration of the Sabbath was a joyous one which elevated concentration on the ethical principles of Judaism. The ultimate idea was the creation of hope for a brighter future when the "eternal Sabbath" would dawn for all mankind. The Sabbath ends with the ritual *Habdalah* (pronounced Hav-dah-lah) which means "separation," separation between the joyous Sabbath of spiritual communion and the ordinary mundane concern of the weekdays.

us to the Crescent City, which is full of life and gaiety and bidding fair to remain in the future as it always was in the past "the metropolis of the South."

W.

Letter Number Eight

Charles Wessolowsky to Rabbi Edward B. M. Browne

Morgan City, Louisiana
27 March 1879

• • •

[*Wessolowsky travels from New Orleans to Morgan City,
Louisiana, in which live approximately fifteen Jewish families;
he praises the religious devotion of the community, describes
their temple, mentions their rabbi, and lauds the active Sunday
school.*]

• • •

"*There is a time for everything,*" saith Solomon; and Wednesday the 26th being the time appointed for my departure from
New Orleans, for the State of Texas, I found myself in readiness early in the morning to answer to the call of the cabman,
reaching the depot of the Morgan Texas Railroad line. We were
conveyed by boat over to Algiers and from thence by cars to
Morgan City, nothing special transpiring on the way, worthy of our
notice; we passed our time with reading, and occasionally looking
out, beholding the husbandman, plowing and breaking up the rich
bottom lands, fulfilling the command: "In the sweat of thy brow
thou shall eat thy bread." At noon we reached Morgan City, a place
of about two thousand inhabitants, an island and which, as I have
learned, is the shipping, or the grand thoroughfare for Texas. By
appointment we stopped here and soon met Rev. Mr. A. Meyer,
formerly of Chattanooga, who brought and introduced me to our
brethren whom we found to be a clever set, and number about
fifteen Jewish families and in all, about one hundred and twenty-
five souls. They are all engaged in mercantile business and doing
well.

Though small in number, they have not forgotten that they also
have a duty to perform as Israelites, and as parents to their children,
and like in Meridian, Miss., they were determined here upon this
island to erect a house wherein they can teach their children "the
unity of God," and demonstrate their teaching by their work. Thus,
they have a handsome small synagogue costing them about four

thousand dollars, wherein divine services are held every sabbath, and to the credit of the Yehudim [Hebrews] of Morgan City may it be said, that on Friday eve, every store is closed, and divine worship attended by all. The officers of the congregation are as follows: Leon Kahn, President; Leopold Loeb (formerly officiating minister), Vice-President; A. Mose, Secretary; and Rev. A. Meyer, minister. The latter in his function is doing a great deal of good, and is a gentleman who is anxious and working energetically for the progress of Judaism and could a larger field be offered to him, we feel assured that his labor would meet that desired success which it deserves.

We regretted to see that no ladies' society of any kind was organized on the island and although, they in their individual capacity are performing a great deal of good, yet I think, a society formed by all the Jewish ladies of Morgan City could indeed be of great benefit to the cause of Judaism.

It is with great reluctance that I revive the memory of the late epidemic, but I cannot refrain from mentioning, that while we have heard of so many *heroes* in various places where the fever was raging, that here a heroine is to be found, who in the late struggle with the "yellow jack" has indeed immortalized herself by her constant work in caring and nursing for the sick. Madame Louis Guggenheim had worked fifty-eight weeks long, and by her administering promptly and faithfully to all requirements saved all, except two.

This we thought certainly deserves a special mention (as we have nothing greater to offer her) and we hope that Madame Louis will pardon us, for giving this matter publicity which we think ought to have been done by someone ere this.

We remained in Morgan City until the following noon, and then embarked on the steamer *Harlan* for Galveston.

We met on the boat Mr. C. Lazard of Calvert, with whom we spent most of our time, and indeed a pleasant trip of it, until next morning when the groaning of one early riser saying, "I have never been sick before"; another remarking, "it is the coffee that made me sick"; a gentleman, somewhat feeling badly is carried to his berth by his wife, others not at the breakfast table (myself included) reminded me that Neptune had somewhat aroused his anger and passion and demanding our homage, which we cheerfully gave, by lying down upon our couch humiliating ourselves and feeling that after all, it takes little to prostrate him who at times may think that he is a giant.

By 9 o'clock, we landed, stepped upon the soil of the Lone Star State, and soon were conveyed to our hotel in the city of Galveston.

W.

Letter Number Nine

Charles Wessolowsky to Rabbi Edward B. M. Browne

Brenham, Texas
6 April 1879

• • •

[*Wessolowsky notes the health measures being taken by the authorities in Galveston, Texas, to prevent the future outbreaks of Yellow Fever epidemics; notes the financial success of Galveston's Jews and their willingness to engage in charitable activities; describes the operation of the Sunday School; mentions the 125 families' involvement in men's and women's benevolent societies, B'nai B'rith, as well as in a Harmony Club for social activity; and he is particularly impressed with the number of Jewish professionals.*]

• • •

We arrived at Galveston, and soon beheld a city full of life, bustle, activity and commercial outlet for the state of Texas. Phoenix-like this city, which but a few years ago numbered about 15,000 is now the large, beautiful *Island City* with about 45,000 inhabitants, is certainly one of the largest cotton ports in the United States. Galveston, with her mammoth business houses, extensive and most beautiful cotton exchange (the handsomest in the United States) other beautiful and elegant structures, magnificent churches, schoolhouses, and places of amusements, bids fair to become in the future a rival of New Orleans, and is certainly in regard to cleanliness. The adoption of wholesome sanitary measures and the precautionary steps taken by all concerned, to prevent the importation of epidemics, are by far superior. The chief aim of her officers, those having the affair of the city in charge, seem to be only to promote the health, prosperity and welfare of her citizens, and if other and neighboring cities would imitate her work and follow her footsteps, many happy homes would not be made desolate, and many, many lives would be spared, as all who today may be at variance and differ, in regard to the cause and origin of the great destroyer of human lives of yellow fever, yet they agree that cleanliness is certainly one of the preventative antidotes against it and all other diseases.

We were pleased to see that our Israelitish brethren are adding vastly to the progress, advancement and promotion of the city, and in fact as to its commercial standing and extensive houses, they are the first and foremost in the city, such large and mammoth commercial firms as L. & H. Blum, S. Heidenheimer & Co., G. Rauger & Co., Lasker & Co., Greenleave, Block & Co., Bernstein & Co., and others too numerous to mention, representing all branches of commercial industry each doing business by the millions, are seldom to be found in any city South, and are an honor and pride to our race. There are others not alone great in the commercial world, but also in their nobility of character, their liberality and abundant charity which they bestow upon all worthy of their attention and aid. It is here where the Hon. Mr. Peixotte received $3,500 in support of the Union College,[53] and where all calls for charity are so loudly and ably responded to. It is also here where humanity and harmony in the fullest term and among all our brethren exists; no distinction of nationality and no preference on account of their millions, all seem to be like brothers, work in common, for all that is elevating, noble and generous, and for the cause of Judaism.

Thus we find a large Congregation with a beautiful Temple and a magnificent choir, led by Mrs. Spier, and a divine worship well attended. The officers of the Congregation B'nai Israel[54] are as follows: President, F. Half; Vice-President, L. C. Michael of the firm of Greenleave, Bloch & Co., Rev. A. Blum the officiating minister. This gentleman in his ministerial functions, is doing a vast deal of good by establishing Sunday Schools in the country places, where there are no ministers and is executing the mission which the *Union* promised to do,[55] and we were pleased to meet him. We

---

[53]The Union College refers to Hebrew Union College, the seminary for the training of rabbis in America. It is the oldest rabbinical seminary in the United States and was one of the chief goals of the formation of the U. A. H. C. Indeed, the formation of the Union by Isaac Mayer Wise was but a means to the creation of a seminary. Hebrew Union College formally opened its doors on 3 October 1875 in Cincinnati. On 24 April 1881, its first permanent home was dedicated, and on 11 July 1883 it graduated its first class of ordained rabbis.

[54]*B'nai Israel* means "sons of Israel" (also see note 41).

[55]The concept of a "circuit-riding" rabbi at that time was a revolutionary one. It was not until the late 1880s that U. A. H. C. took up this issue. It was not until 1895 that the Committee on Circuit-Preaching successfully developed a circuit-preaching plan. See Fox, "On the Road to Unity," pp. 186-88.

visited his Sunday School, numbering about 150 pupils, addressed the children and found them in all respects advanced in religious studies. The reverend gentleman takes a pride in his Sunday School, and is aided in teaching by Mrs. Pierce, Miss I.C. Levy and other young ladies, whose names we do not remember. He also has a daily Hebrew School which we were prevented from visiting,[56] but learned that the children were advancing rapidly.

There is also a Hebrew Benevolent Society here, dispensing charities to all who call upon them—which is mostly done by parties from abroad—as Galveston, indeed, is fortunate; I know that among the 125 families residing there, there is perhaps but one family who may be forced to ask for aid. This Society, I learn, had contributed a great deal toward alleviating the wants and necessities of the yellow fever sufferers, and is the pride of all the Yehudim [Hebrews] in the city. Mr. L. Lovenberg is President, and J. Hostein, Vice-President—two gentlemen ever ready to perform all duties appertaining to their office. This society was established in 1865. Mr. J. W. Frank, was the first president of the congregation, being also the first president of the Society, and deservedly does the gentleman feel proud of his labors.

Our Jewish ladies here have not neglected their duties and, like true mothers in Israel, are furthering the aims and objects of our mission, and are doing all for the promotion and elevation of Judaism. They have a Ladies' Hebrew Benevolent Society, the officers as follows: President, Mrs. J. Block; Vice-President, Mrs. Julia Marx; Secretary, Mrs. Rev. H. Blum; Treasurer, Mrs. I. C. Levy. This society co-operates with the other Hebrew Benevolent Society, and is of great service to the needy.

A B'nai B'rith Lodge, named after the immortal Zacharia Frankel,[57] numbering about ninety members, has also been

---

[56]In 1874 U. A. H. C. established a Committee on Sabbath Schools for the purpose of publishing texts, making suggestions to member congregations, and helping to establish Sunday Schools. One of the strongest suggestions was that of hiring teachers fluent in the English language. Many of the rabbis, including Rabbi Blum whom Wessolowsky mentions utilized the offices of U. A. H. C. for the purpose of setting up Sunday schools on their circuit. See Fox, "On the Road to Unity," pp. 182-85.

[57]Zacharia Frankel, 1801-1887, was born in Prague. A moderate reformer, he

established here, and is in a flourishing condition. Its officers are: President, Bro. C. A. Miller, Vice-President, Bro. Jacob Sonnentheil; Secretary, Bro. Leopold Weiss; Treasurer, I. Lovenberg. Upon invitation, we lectured in the Lodge, and found them to be proficient in the works of the Order.

Last, but not least, is also to be found here a "Harmony Club," with Mr. Albert Weis as President, and L. Weis as Secretary. With a "weis" man as its head officer, and a "weis" man as its scribe, we doubt not that *Harmony* must prevail, and its aims are strictly carried out—This club was instituted for the bodily and mental enjoyment of its members, and seems to be visited by them quite often.

Galveston also boasts of Jewish notaries, lawyers, bankers, and gentlemen of other high standing, and in all, our Israelitish brethren here are, in every regard, honored and respected. Their active minister, Mr. Blum, has been but lately elected as President of the Medical College.

Our stay in that city has been marked by courtesies and kind offices shown to us. We passed our time pleasantly, and were pleased to meet our friend and countryman, Mr. I. C. Levy, who has placed us under many obligations.

Thus we remained here until Friday morning, when we took the train up to Houston and there changed for Brenham on the Central Road, where we arrived that noon. More in our next.

C. W.

---

was the founder of the "positivist-historical" school in Breslau. His thinking greatly influenced the later conservative movement in the United States. He taught that changes should be effected in Jewish ritual only if they did not conflict with the spirit of historical Judaism. That is, that ritual which was directly connected with Mosaic origins should be left unaltered.

Letter Number Ten

Charles Wessolowsky to Rabbi Edward B. M. Browne

> Brenham and Hempstead,
> Texas
> April 1879

• • •

[*In Brenham, Wessolowsky talks of the German colony of
settlers, fourteen families of which are Jewish; he bemoans
their disunity and religious disinterest; he chastises them,
particularly the women, for neglecting the religious education
of the children; in contrast, in Hempstead he applauds the
attempt of the small Jewish community to perpetuate their
religion; and publicly urges, rhetorically, the Jews of Russia
and Rumania to "colonize" the Texas plains.*]

• • •

Brenham, a small city of about four or five thousand
inhabitants, and situated on a branch of the Central road, is the
county site [seat] of Washington county, and seems to be a fine
business point. It is the market for those German immigrants who
have settled in these parts and formed a German colony. We were
indeed surprised to hear so much of the German and Polish
language spoken here, and had it not been that occasionally the
American Eagle, extending the wings of protection to all was
visible, and here and there an English sentence sounded on our ears,
we would have believed ourselves to be in some part of Western
Prussia, on the line of Poland, giving attention to a *Benkannt-
machung* [notification], and paying our respects to a *wachmeister*
[police sergeant] or *burgermeister* [mayor].

The German farmers as a class are also prospering and utilizing
the Texas fertile soil to their advantage. Their habits, mode of
living, custom and costume are the same to which they were
addicted in Germany, and the women even wear dresses made of the
German *Nessel*.[58]

---

[58]The *Nessel* (or nettle) was a traditional pattern that was woven into many
traditional German costumes.

Great Bohemians are also settled around here, and I am told they as well as the other emigrants make excellent law-abiding citizens, which, after all, is their second nature, and is peculiar to all foreigners within this country.

Within this place we found about fourteen Jewish families and a population of about one hundred and fifty souls. They are all engaged in mercantile pursuits and apparently are doing well.

But we regret exceedingly that we are forced to say that we found no unity nor sociability among them. Every one seems to live within himself, and for himself, always believing and thinking how mean and low his neighbor is.

They seem to forget their higher and nobler mission on this earth; and are every ready to perceive the faults of others, without one moment's inquiry "*Am I any better?*" Matters pertaining to Judaism (save a B. B. Lodge, which, as far as we could ascertain, is not the type of "unity" nor the symbol of Brotherly love) are entirely neglected by them, and thus we found Jewish children regularly attending "Christian" Sunday School, to receive the most useful instruction that Jesus is the "*Saviour of all mankind.*" We found among them all but one noble widow lady, who seems to realize this deplorable state of affairs, and she even offered her services to the other parents as a religious teacher, being fully capable of instructing, but met with no success. And when we demonstrated to some of our mothers in Israel, the danger and evil that may arise to those children from such an intercourse, we were met with the blunt answer, "they did not think so," and seemed not to care. Ah, parents, had we the opportunity, we would say unto you that after all, the *Golden Calf* is not *thy God, O Israel*, and that we, as parents, have a higher and more serious duty to perform than simply to be enwrapped in business, to accumulate wealth for our children, which, perhaps, may be the cause of their ruin, and the stimulant to their vice and evil, which may bring disgrace and shame upon us. You, as daughters of *Sarah* and Rebecca,[59] ought never to forget that it is your sacred duty as well, to instruct your children, to give them a religious and moral training, and that the lessons which you

[59]Rebecca (as wife of Isaac and mother of Jacob), and Sarah (as wife of Abraham and mother of Isaac) are considered to be the matriarchs of the Jewish people.

impress upon them in their youth, and in the way you train them while young, will ever remain with them, and they will not depart from it when old, remember that there is a great debt of responsibility resting upon you, and that you are held accountable to a great extent for the acts of your children. It is our duty to teach our children by example, and to extend our usefulness, influence and energy in aiding them to receive the moral and religious instructions of our unbiased and truthful religion. Ah, indeed! Had we the opportunity we could clearly bring before you facts and living testimonies, where such grave errors as committed by you have brought destruction to children, and broken hearts to parents. Alas, we had none, and we take this occasion to remind you of the danger, that underlies the course that you are pursuing; and we trust that our Israelite brethren will pardon us for being that frank with them, as we deem it our duty and our most sacred obligation to bring the above facts to their notice. We do this in behalf of Judaism, in behalf of the future welfare of its children, and are only executing the mission which our public life has imposed on us.

We remained here several days, spent the first days of Pesach [Passover] with Mrs. Peters, who bestowed us many courtesies, for which we return thanks to her and all those who made our stay pleasant.

Wednesday evening we took the train for Hempstead, where we arrived in due time and were the guest of Mr. Cohen. Here we met the learned Rev. Mr. Schwartz, with whom we spent a few hours, and found him very agreeable. The Israelites here although they have not yet acquired a synagogue hold worship in a hall on Pesach and are trying to perpetuate the faith of their fathers. We lectured that night in the courthouse to a very attentive audience, and received the appreciation of our brethren and Christian friends, for which we are very grateful.

This place, although somewhat smaller than Brenham, affords large business houses and we find here some of our brethren carrying on quite an extensive business and others are also engaged in agricultural pursuits. This brings to us the idea, how well it would be for some of our Jewish brethren living in those barbarous countries of Russia and Rumania to immigrate here to Texas, form Jewish colonies, on this fertile soil pursue the avocation of our forefathers, become shepherds like Moses and David. Here in these prairies, where I am told, stock business is very remunerative and prosperous, let them throw off their Russian shackles and Rumanian fetters and come here to this land of liberty and be a blessing to themselves and to this country, where millions of uncultivated acres cry out for immigration, civilization and progress. Let them come here, rid themselves of the yoke of oppression, enjoy the freedom of our country, establish schools, secure enlightenment and advancement, and thereby enrich themselves and this country. Would this not be a thought for the Union to reflect upon?

Friday morning bidding adieu to our worthy host and hostess, we departed for the city of Houston, where we arrived at nine o'clock and soon met Rev. Dr. Voorsaenger, who insisted upon us to be his guest,[60] which we cheerfully accepted.

C. W.

---

[60]Rabbi Voorsaenger was to be Wessolowsky's successor as associate editor of the Jewish South. See *Jewish South*, 5 August 1881.

Letter Number Eleven

Charles Wessolowsky to Rabbi Edward B. M. Browne

Houston, Texas
April 1879

• • •

[*Wessolowsky notes that there are 75 Jewish families living in Houston; he mentions that most of them are engaged in business activities with some professionals among them, a few hold high political position in the city government; he discusses the character of Jacob Voorsaenger, the congregation's Rabbi; he describes the operation of the Sunday School which is attended by over one hundred children; and he talks of the charity balls put on by the Hebrew Ladies Benevolent Society.*]

• • •

When Texas rebelled against Mexico, fighting for liberty and free government, a Georgian named Faunie left his home, to join in the struggle for freedom; but the career of this noble Georgian was short. His army was massacred, and he, refusing the offer of life upon the stipulation of kneeling, preferring death to dishonor, was also basely shot. A General Houston was then called to take command of the Texas army, and he, by his bravery, military skill, at the decisive battle of San Jacinto, aided vastly in achieving the liberties for the Texans, and was afterwards elected President of the Republic.

To perpetuate his memory, this city is named after him, and how would the heart of this illustrious general beat for joy, if he could rise from his tomb and behold the spot, which but a short period ago perhaps was barren, today is adorned with elegant structures, magnificent buildings, handsome edifices, and with everything in face that entitles "Houston to be classed a beautiful city." Alas such is the fate of man, we toil, we plant our hopes, but others reap and realize them.

The appearance of Houston indeed has somewhat startled us, as we did not anticipate to find such a large, handsome city, with all modern improvements and grand public buildings which would be an honor and credit to a larger city than Houston, which numbers about thirty thousand inhabitants.

Among those, we find five hundred Jewish souls and about seventy-five families, following their avocation in life, some in mercantile pursuits, others in banking business, political life, or they are professional men. Our people here can boast of wealth, talent, prominence and are much respected by the Gentiles. We find here Jewish bankers, lawyers, and merchants doing extensive and large business in all branches of commerce, and even the city clerk and treasurer is a Jew—holding that position for about nine years, with credit to himself and pride to our people.

The congregation with the banker, H. S. Fox, as its president; the price merchant, A. Harris, as its vice-president; is in a flourishing condition—Rev. Dr. Voorsaenger who is the minister, is doing all in his power to build up and elevate Judaism, and with his eloquence and learning, he succeeds to have a full attendance of Jew and Gentile to the Friday evening service. The Doctor is indeed one of the few fine English Jewish pulpit orators, and his lectures are admired and listened to, with all attention—He is very much honored by the Gentiles of Houston, and, but lately has been elected president of a society, composed mostly of Christians, and has been appointed by them as the English orator for the *Volksfest* [state festival]; well may his congregation be proud of him, and we feel satisfied that his continual labors in Houston will advance the cause of Judaism, not alone in his city, but everywhere, where his ringing voice is heard, and his eloquence listened to. We feel that we could say much more in behalf of this "Demosthenes," but we fear that we might shock his modesty, and therefore will forgo the pleasure.

We visited his Sunday School, numbering about one hundred pupils and were indeed delighted to find such decorum and behavior among them. The Doctor is the Superintendent and Mrs. Dr. Larenden, Principal. They are aided by the following teachers: Misses Sallie Jacobs, Harriet Levy, Eva Solomon, Isabella Rosenfield, Emma Levy, and Messrs. J. Louis Souza and Isaac Gerson, all have their respective classes, and we found the children well versed in their studies.

Upon the request of the Doctor we addressed the children who seem to have been pleased with what we told them. But what we found new and novel to us, was the Choir selected from the Sunday School scholars who conducted the Sabbath morning services with such regularity and credit to themselves that we indeed felt proud of them, and wish that many of our ministers would follow this move of obtaining a choir, so that we at once can do away with Gentiles chanting our *Schema Israel*[61] and thereby aid congregations in diminishing the expenses. The choir for the evening services aided by Mrs. Raphael and Messrs. Reichman and E. Raphael, all excellent singers, is very fine and makes the services very attractive.

We were pleased to meet Mrs. Spiers, the "Galveston Nightingale," who also sang in the choir at last Friday night services and who is here to take part in the presentation of the opera comique "The Doctor of Alcantara," given for the benefit of a young lady from Houston now in Europe to finish her musical education. We know that with such cast of characters: E. Raphael as the Dr. Paracelisus; John Reichman as Don Pomposa; Mrs. Spiers as Donna Lucrezis, and others of like fame, the result must be very beneficial and the success complete. It is a laudable undertaking and no doubt the people of Houston will patronize it liberally.

The B'nai B'rith Lodge "Lone Star" has a large membership and is working harmoniously. We attended a meeting, addressed the brothers and were satisfied with their work.

The Hebrew Ladies Benevolent Society are anxious and zealous in their charity and benevolence, gave a calico ball for the purpose of swelling their treasury, to which we have been honored with a "complimentary ticket." We attended the same, spent an enjoyable evening and were delighted with the entertainment. The dazzling beauties of the ladies there assembled, their tasty and beautiful attire, their elegant and splendid figure have put us to thinking whether there are any handsomer ladies in Georgia or elsewhere, and we came to the conclusion that with the exception of one (of course my wife) they cannot be surpassed. The entertainment was given in the Turner Hall; below, a large and commodious hall for

---

[61]*Schema Israel* literally means "Hear, O Israel." This declaration taken from Deut. 4:9, expresses the supreme declaration of the Jewish belief in God's unity and sovereignty. It is the fundamental truth of Judaism. It is the basis of the Jewish creed and the basis of Jewish life. The entire passage embodies the duty of Judaism that was to be constantly impressed in memory. It enshrines the fundamental dogma of Judaism, monotheism; the fundamental duty, love; the fundamental discipline, study of the law; and the fundamental method, ritual. Israel Abrahams, *A Companion to the Authorised Daily Prayerbook* (New York: Hermon Press, 1966).

dancing, and upstairs the society has a restaurant where the most fastidious could find something to satisfy their palates.

The excitement of the evening was the raffle of some handsome cakes, to the most popular young, and married ladies—and Miss Eva Solomon, as the popular young lady, and Mrs. Sam Jacobs as the popular married lady, carried off the prizes to the satisfaction of all.

The affair was quite a success, though not as largely patronized as it ought to have been and we were somewhat surprised not to find a great number of gentlemen there, as the cause is worthy, noble, and those ladies certainly deserved a full and liberal patronage, unless some of our pious men, were perhaps frightened away by the presence and sale of "ham,"[62] which they thought ought not to have been at an entertainment given by the Hebrew Ladies Benevolent Society. The officers of this society are: Mrs. Felix Woolf, President; Mrs. Dr. Larendon, Vice-President; Mrs. Admons, Secretary; Mrs. Morris Levy, Treasurer. We hope that their labors may forever be crowned with success, and that unity and good feelings shall prevail among them.

There is also a Y.M.H.A., here, with Mr. E. Raphael as its president—we cannot give any particulars, nor the aim and object of this association, as we had not the opportunity of ascertaining the same—this association invited us to deliver a lecture which we did at the temple on Wednesday night to a fair and appreciative audience. Our country-man D. G. Rosenfield has placed us under many obligations for courtesies bestowed upon us.

We also met Dr. L. Heidingfelder, the celebrated mohel,[63] who,

---

[62]The item of food which always comes to mind when the laws of *kosher* are discussed is the prohibition against eating ham or any other pork product. Actually, the prohibition is against eating any animal with cloven hooves. Obviously, from Wessolowsky's comments, the members of Galveston's Jewish community had not entirely shed themselves of adherence to the dietary laws so that it caused some friction between those who observed and those who did not.

[63]*Mohel* (pronounced moy-el) is the circumciser who performs the operation of circumcision upon the Jewish male child on the eighth day of his life. The custom stems from God's command to Abraham in Gen. 17:1-14 and a traditional belief that the prophet Elijah is witness to the ritual. The ceremony is an occasion for rejoicing and great celebration.

it seems is continually on the road to answer the calls made upon him.

Our stay in Houston was made very pleasant and agreeable, and we return thanks to all of our friends, who have treated us so kindly. Wednesday morning we were again on the wing and took the train for San Antonio.

C. W.

Letter Number Twelve

Charles Wessolowsky to Rabbi Edward B. M. Browne

Columbus, Lulino, and
San Antonio, Texas
April 1879

• • •

[*Wessolowsky briefly mentions the existence of a B'nai B'rith Lodge in Columbus, Texas, that is supported by that town's twelve Jewish families; he offers passing comments on the small Jewish community of about ten families in Lulino, Texas; he gives a brief history of San Antonio, Texas; he offers comments on a Catholic service he attended and compares it to a Jewish service; he describes the temple built by San Antonio's thirty-five Jewish families; he describes the Jewish economic and social life; on returning to Columbus, he attends a B'nai B'rith Lodge meeting where he gave a lecture and attended an after-meeting social.*]

• • •

Tuesday morning we left Houston for San Antonio, but stopped at Columbus, where we found about twelve Jewish families and a number of young men who were all in full anticipation of glee and joy, as next Sunday was the time appointed for Naomi Lodge of I. O. B. B. to be instituted. We had to promise that we would return then and aid in the work, to which Bro. E. Raphael the Grand V. P., and Bro. Richman, both from Houston, will be present. Thus, we did not tarry long, and left with the first freight for Lulino, another small place of some importance about thirty-five miles from San Antonio. This little city has about the same number of Jewish families as Columbus, and although quite a new place, yet is being built up rapidly, and is making progress. We were pleased to meet Mr. Miller, the junior partner of the firm Epstein and Miller, who aided us very much in our work at Lulino, and who accompanied us on our way to San Antonio, where we arrived Wednesday evening.

This city possesses a charm that attracts the attention of the stranger, and inspired the pens of many historians. This ancient city as old as Philadelphia, known as the place where the blood of patriots and martyrs was freely spilled, and the sacred Alamo with its historic record now standing as a relic of old, and of the chivalrous past, is indeed an object of admiration, and claims to be the metropolis of the great South-West.

This Alamo, or the Thermopylae of Texas,[64] originally built on the Rio Grande in 1703 and subsequently moved to various other places and in 1741 transferred to its present location on Alamo Plaza, where from the date of battle until the annexation of the Republic of Texas to the United States of America was used by the Army of the Republic, and from then used for the United States Army Quartermasters Department, until recently when the Alamo and adjoining buildings were sold and is now used for a storehouse for groceries.

There are also other places of attraction such as the Mission Churches established here by adventurers who first visited this country and those who were seeking to extend the Christian religion—thus the period during which the Spaniards occupied Texas, 1690 to the Mexican Revolution in 1820, is called "The Mission Period." The mission was conducted by monks of various orders, the Catholic religion planted and chapels built which also were to answer for fortress in case of danger. Indians of various tribes were converted, baptized and placed in the happy state of being able to enter the celestial kingdom. There are a great number of those missions in and around San Antonio, some of which are now ruins, and others are preserved in a good state. San Fernandes, the so-called mission in San Antonio, was built in 1732. In 1868 it was rebuilt as a cathedral, a portion of the old walls in the rear of the new building forms the sacristy of the present church occupied by the Spanish speaking population of San Antonio, and is a very commodious and attractive building. We saw Mass celebrated by some present, and we hope that our orthodox friends[65] will forgive

---

[64]This reference is to the battle in which 500 Spartans fought a successful but sacrificing holding action against the Persian invaders around the beginning of the fifth century B.C.E.

[65]Orthodox, literally meaning "true opinion," was the traditional Judaism that developed and grew out of the Middle Ages and against which Reform Judaism emerged at the end of the 18th century. Conservative Judaism appeared in the United States at the end of the 19th century at a position between Orthodox and Reform Judaism.

us of having entered this Catholic church and remained in it all the forenoon on Sunday, as curiosity, (and thinking that we will hear a good sermon preached by some divine,) bade us enter, and we were indeed astonished to see that many intelligent men and women were keeping up steadfastly their old ceremonies, bowing before an idol[66] and crowding the church, which has a capacity of holding perhaps about one thousand people or more, and yet our gorgeous temples, teaching the religion of light, where no symbols, no images, or likeness of a deity, is to be found, but simply the ten commandments, and over it perhaps the infallible name:[67] wherein we address ourselves entirely to the human intelligence, and cannot use any of those religious paraphernalia, are but so seldom entered and by very few visited. I asked myself, why is this? Our edifices are just as handsome and beautiful, our choir producing music just as sweetly, our services certainly as attractive, and why do we enter our Temples on Saturday morning and perhaps, cannot find ten male persons?[68] Echo answers, why?

---

[66]The "idol" to which Wessolowsky referred was obviously an image of Jesus. For knowledgeable Jews, the Christian iconography and statuary always posed a problem revolving around both the issues of idolatry and the finite representation of God. Indeed, the major stumbling block was the concept of the Trinity which was viewed by many rabbis as a simple corruption of Judaic monotheism by pagan polytheism.

[67]The Jews could never understand attempts to anthropomorphize God. The synagogue and temple are completely void of any imagery, although in Reform temples the imagery of a human being is permitted. In many conservative and orthodox synagogues even human imagery, because of the divine spark that exists in man, is prohibited. For Judaism, God is beyond man's capacity to know. Of God, man can at best claim to believe in the existence of God. Nothing that exists within God's realm, as Job concludes, is comprehensible to man. God has no likeness that can be carved or painted. There are no symbols that can depict or refer to God. Even God's reference is unpronouncible—YWHW. The only imagery that is permitted in the sanctuary of any temple or synagogue is the eternal light referring to the Covenant, the tablets of the Ten Commandments referring to the law, and other symbols depicting major events in biblical lore—pillar of fire, blessing of the hands, lions, tree of knowledge, wailing wall, dove, etc.

[68]According to tradition, a quorum of ten men is required for a ritual service to be performed and for certain prayers to be uttered. This quorum is called a *minyan* (pronounced min-yan). Exceptions to the requirement for the presence of a quorum are weddings and circumcisions.

This city numbers about ten thousand inhabitants and among them we find about thirty-five Jewish families, and about two hundred and fifty Jewish souls. Our Israelites here are doing a very extensive business, and some of them are indeed great rivals of the king merchants of Galveston, Messrs. Goldfrank and Frank, Half and Co., Z. Oppenheimer & Co., and others too numerous to mention, are doing business by the millions, and are very much respected in the mercantile world.

A splendid temple, costing about twenty-five thousand dollars, decorates the city, but I regret to say, the congregation has no officiating minister, and we hope that ere long, the thrilling voice of some good pulpit orator will be heard therein, expounding the doctrines of Judaism, and that with his true eloquence, and by his good example and deeds will elevate the same. Mr. S. Mayers, who is President of the Congregation, will certainly spare no trouble in finding that minister who will bestow honor upon Judaism in this Catholic city.

There is also a B. B. Lodge in good condition, Bro. Mayers as president and Bro. Siechel, secretary.

We have not the pleasure of being able to record of the existence of any ladies society, and we feel that by a little infusion of spirit and a determination by some of our Jewish ladies, to institute a society, whereby they can accomplish so much good; the same can be fanned into life, and be a living monument to our Jewish ladies in San Antonio. Through the courtesy of Michael Bros., we enjoyed a ride through the city beholding all that is noteworthy in this old Spanish place and also a visit to the San Pedro Springs, a beautiful place of resort about three miles distant, here Jew and Gentile engage their Sunday evening, hearing fine music and indulging in other pleasures, and are not oppressed by the existing "Sunday Laws," or fears of being indicted for any such offense, created by puritan law makers. We return our best thanks to those gentlemen and to others, who aid in making our stay pleasant.

We were also pleased to meet Messrs. Berg Bros. originally from Savannah, Ga., who are enjoying a good reputation and are doing a prosperous business here.

The heavy rains prevented the fulfillment of our promise to return to Columbus for Sunday and thus we were forced to remain here until Tuesday morning, when we took the train for that city and arrived there at noon.

Upon our arrival we soon learned that the memorial Sunday for the Jews of Columbus, was a day of joy and festivity. On that day the long anticipated pleasure, of being united into one common brotherhood, and brought into the folds of the order of B'nai B'rith had been realized. Naomi Lodge was instituted by Bros. V. P. Raphael, Richman, and others. Our brethren in Columbus, today, reap the fruits of their labors of past years and like Columbus, although encountering many storms upon their voyage, much unpleasantness and trial of life during their passage, today, they see their long dreams of ideas of progress brought into life, and the name of Judaism planted, the banner of B. B. in their midst, which I trust will ever wave for Israel and Humanity.

Your correspondent from Hallettsville having given a full description of the institution, festival and election of officers, I will forgo the pleasure of repeating the same and will only mention that we indeed feel sorry of having been deprived of being in their midst on the day of memorial, and also from participating of their festivities which we learned were on a grand scale and to the satisfaction of all. Upon invitation we lectured to them on Tuesday night, upon the tenets of the order, and next day after bidding adieu to our host and hostess Mr. and Mrs. Rosenfield and our friends, we left Columbus with Mr. Ehrenwerth and returned to Houston, where we remained overnight, attended a concert, upon invitation of friend Rosenfield, listened to the charming music and elegant singing, which indeed was heavenly and when we inquired who it was, giving us that pleasure, not having program handy, why we were told it is our Galveston nightingale, Mrs. Spiers. We were more than rejoiced to see her receiving so many recognitions of appreciation, and that the audience too, felt as we did, that she is deserving of all.

Mrs. Steinbach, also another Jewish lady, was applauded very much for her excellent performing on the piano. Mrs. Steinbach is known as a celebrated artist, and her playing meets with the universal appreciation.

In the morning we took the central train for Navasato, to see our bright little correspondent "Gussie,"[69] and we landed there at noon.

C.W.

P.S. Our friend Rev. Dr. Voorsaenger met us at the depot and we were pleased to see him in full bloom of life. The Rev. gentleman, we learn, will soon be called to various places in Texas to institute Sunday Schools.

C.W.

---

[69]"Gussie" is an example of the type of pseudonym the volunteer stringers for the *Jewish South* adopted in the course of their correspondence.

Letter Number Thirteen

Charles Wessolowsky to Rabbi Edward B. M. Browne

Navasota, Giddings, and
Austin, Texas
May 1879

• • •

[*Wessolowsky praises the harmony that prevails within the Jewish community of Navasota, Texas; in Giddings, Texas, he found eight Jewish families; in Austin, Texas, the thirty-five Jewish families have recently purchased land on which to build a temple; they have no rabbi, but have recently begun a Sunday School that is operated by the women; he describes the activites of the Jewish charitable organizations; and he identifies two Jewish past Grand Masters of the Odd Fellows of Texas.*]

• • •

Navasota, though a small place of about two thousand inhabitants, and with no special attraction or admiration for a stranger, yet to us it was of great charm and beauty, as we found here the realization and true meaning of those words of the Bard "How good and how pleasant it is for brethren to dwell together in unity." There are about ten Jewish families here, perhaps in all about 60 souls. All of them are employed in their daily avocation of life, working in their mercantile business to the best advantages and profits of their own. Yet they represent the true picture of union, harmony and sociability. Each one speaks well of his neighbor, considers him his square man, entitled to his sympathies and well-wishes, and the neighbor in return bestows upon him his kind and generous feeling, ever ready to extend his might to make it pleasant and sociable, and thus they dwell in peace, are happy and enjoy the blessing of life. What a contrast to the picture which we beheld in other places. How pleasant and agreeable our brothers everywhere could live if only such feelings would prompt them and they would be aroused to the knowledge that we are all brothers, that we all have but one Father.

Our brothers here intend to start a B. B. Lodge and Sunday School, we know that with their harmonious feeling and work, their institution will progress and be prosperous.

We were pleased to meet the handsome blond, "Our Little Gussie," the spicy contributor to our children's department [of *The Jewish South*], she being only about thirteen years of age, yet is very tall, and is indeed very far advanced in her studies. We bespeak for her a promising bright future and may she continue ever to remain the pride and honor of her parents, the pleasure and joy of all who know her.

We remained in Navasota only a short while, as we were forced to meet our appointments elsewhere, and with a pleasing impression of the place and of our brothers, we left next morning for Giddings, where we arrived at three o'clock in the evening, and became the guest of Mr. and Mrs. Alexander. Upon our arrival, we were invited to attend a picnic, which was a drill two miles from the city. There we met Jew and Gentile, enjoying the rural pleasures, and we soon had occasion to be introduced to all our Israelites, whom indeed, we found to be clever and pleasant. We also met here, our friend Miss Fannie Cohen, from Hempstead, and Miss Julia Cohen from Dallas, and were delighted to see them. After spending a few hours pleasantly, we returned to the city to enjoy the comforts of my host and hostess.

Giddings numbers about twelve hundred inhabitants, among whom we find about eight Jewish families and about fifty souls. They are all in good condition and seem to follow the life of our Navasota Yehudim [Hebrews]. The city boasts of an elegant courthouse, which is about the only handsome building in the place.

Here we remained over Sunday, enjoying the hospitalities so lavishly bestowed upon us, and Monday noon we took the train for the city of Austin, the capital of Texas.

In this place we found ourselves once more in the midst of life and gaiety. Austin has many attractions, and natural, romantic and beautiful sceneries, so that we at once may style her, "the handsome and beautiful city of Texas."

We enjoyed a ride through the city offered to us by the courtesy of Mr. De Cordova, a most affable and polished gentleman; and we had occasion to observe all points and places of splendor and beauty. The elegant private residences, the magnificent public structures of all kind, the handsome capitol building, which is soon to be torn down and replaced by one costing about a million, and the beautiful avenue, all claimed our admiration. We were indeed loud in our utterance of praises and the pleasure we experienced at the sight of all these.

We saw the building used as a kitchen by the first president of the Republic, and which stands today in perfectly good order.

This handsome city numbers about fifteen thousand inhabitants, and we find therein about thirty-five Jewish families, and perhaps two hundred and fifty Jewish souls. All seems to be in good circumstances, doing well and are very much respected among the Gentiles. Many of them are carrying on a vast and extensive business, and some of them are old citizens of Austin, having resided there for the past twenty-six years; and those in particular are enjoying the respect and goodwill of all.

We regret to say that we are unable to record the existence of a handsome temple, as our Israelitish brethren, although having purchased a lot sometime ago for the purpose of erecting a synagogue, have as yet neglected it, or perhaps did not feel themselves strong enough to enter into such an undertaking; but we hope that ere long a gorgeous and handsome edifice erected by the Israelites of Austin, wherein the voice of an eloquent and able minister will be heard for the elevation of Judaism, will beautify and adorn some street of the Capital.

The Sunday School that has been lately established under the call of the *Jewish South*, is progressing finely, and we were pleased to see so much interest taken by all in behalf of its advancement and to make the same interesting and pleasing to the children as well as to all the visitors—Mr. S. Philipson is superintendent—the right man in the right place, and exhibits a willingness and zeal to make the school a perfect success—Mrs. D. Friedman is principal in the female department, Miss Rose Milaski, Bertha Gans, Sarah Davis, Rosa Bieverstein, and Messrs. Ernest Pessels and Joe Marx are its teachers.

It was our pleasure to know the principal, Mrs. Friedman, while she resided in Chattanooga, even then, she worked zealously and energetically in behalf of Judaism, and but lately after her removal to the City of Austin, the Israelites of Chattanooga have rewarded her with a token of appreciation, consisting of a handsome and elegant watercolor with a most appropriate and neat inscription of "Presentation," for her most valuable labors and untiresome efforts in the choirs as well as in the Sunday School in Chattanooga, of which she has been the leader and principal. We congratulate our Israelites in Austin in being so fortunate of having Mrs. F. in their midst, who no doubt, will display the same energy, use the same indefatigable zeal to advance the cause of Judaism as well in Austin, as she did in her former home, and may Mrs. F. remain an ornament in Judaism.

The B. B. Lodge with Bro. A. Goldbaum, as president is working harmoniously and stood the storm of the heavy endowments.

We are deprived of the pleasure of not being able to chronicle the existence of a Hebrew Ladies Society of any kind. Our Jewish ladies in Austin, no doubt, fully understand their duties and all they would need perhaps, is a "reminder."

Bro. S. Hirschfield has placed us under obligations and we return thanks to him and to all who favored us.

We cannot close this letter, without mentioning that our friend Mr. De Cordova, has been Grand Master of the Odd Fellows for the State of Texas, already ten years ago, and while we do not wish to rob our friend Adolph Brandt of the honor of being the first Israelite who ever held that position, according to a statement made in the *Jewish South*, yet impartial justice demands the above correction at our hands, and we trust Bro. Brandt will certainly pardon us.

Thursday morning we left the capital, promising our friends that we will return on Sunday, visit their school and lecture in the B. B. Lodge, and took the train for Rockdale, stopping at Round Rock, where we were pleased to meet Mr. and Mrs. Koppel, our worthy host and hostess during our stay in that city.

We remained there overnight and departed Friday morning for Rockdale, where a committee of brethren awaited our arrival at the depot, and we became the guest of Rockdale Lodge. More anon.

C. W.

Letter Number Fourteen

Charles Wessolowsky to Rabbi Edward B. M. Browne

Rockdale, Palestine,
Hearn, and Calvert, Texas
May 1879

• • •

[*Wessolowsky talks of signs of religious division in the
Rockdale Jewish community between an orthodox minority
and the majority of Reform Jews; in Palestine, he regrets
observing religious indifference and the lack of charitable
activities, as well as the absence of any socializing among the
Jews; he merely mentions the presence of some Jews in Hearn,
Texas; and he discusses an argument that appeared in the
Jewish South regarding the education of the Jewish children in
Calvert, Texas.*]

• • •

We remained in Rockdale Friday and Saturday, were indeed
pleased with our brothers and had a very pleasant and agreeable
time. The Israelites here numbering about one hundred souls and
perhaps fifteen families, seem to be above the average on point of
intelligence and with exception of a few live in harmony and unity.

Rockdale Lodge I.O.B.B., although small in number, yet is
progressing finely, and the president Bro. Lovenstein, whose
untiring zeal and energy has aided so much in keeping up and
maintaining the Lodge, will shortly under its auspices inaugurate a
Sunday School, through it to carry out strictly the teachings "learn
and teach." We know that the brothers belonging to that Lodge will
work faithfully and watch diligently for the interest of Rockdale
Lodge and for the elevation and advancement of Judaism and
thereby aid the Bro. President in accomplishing the long felt
necessity and neglect in small cities, viz. the religious teaching of our
youth.

We lectured in Rockdale to a very fair and appreciative
audience, and trust that we have pleased them.

Our brothers here are all engaged in the mercantile pursuits and
are doing well. The only small division and perhaps unpleasantness
existing among them, is the variance of opinion in regard to the

ceremonial part of our Jewish religion, some of them still cling and hold fast to the doctrines and dead forms of the so-called chasid,[70] while others require and ask for "progress," and to weigh man's action in the scales of reason and not in blind faith and empty and idle ceremonies. We regretted very much to that difference existing, and would say to them "Let not our religion be like a shell without a kernel and let us with the effect and garb of wisdom and intelligence dispel that unfortunate indifference, which is so prevalent with some classes of our people. Let the essence of religious actions be such, that we do not in some instances forget that we are Jews, while in others we believe ourselves to be Saints. Let noble and good impulses prompt us in our action and by the evidence of our work arouse others from lethargy, and make them have a constant yearning for a true and enlightened religion."

We trust that we have not trespassed upon the feelings of our brothers in Rockdale when we allowed ourselves to mention the above facts, and that ere long all these petty differences will be amicably and pleasantly reconciled.

Sunday noon accompanied by many of our brothers we started for the depot, and bidding adieu to all, we took the train for Palestine, having as a traveling companion our friend Elias from Galveston, and arrived in the evening.

From the bustle and life in the street, on Sunday, we thought that we were indeed in Palestine, where Saturday is strictly observed by our people, Sunday, the business day. Alas, upon inquiring we were told that we were mistaken and that in this Palestine no Saturday is kept.

This seems to be a very prosperous city and the home of the superintendent of the International and Great Northern Railroad, who by the erection of machine shops and other elegant buildings is beautifying the city and the increase of workingmen, mechanics and laborers, gives Palestine a healthy growth, and is now a city of about six or seven thousand inhabitants. We enjoyed a ride through the city, through courtesy of our friend Mr. Chas. Jacobs, and we

---

[70]*Chasid* or *Hasid* (pronounced ha-sid) literally means "pietist." The early rabbis used the term to designate a just, upright, and good person who adhered to a higher standard of observance of ritual and moral commandments than most. In modern parlance, as Wessolowsky uses the term, it means "ultraorthodox."

observed that a large number of brick store-houses, beautiful residences are in course of erection and which when finished, will add vastly to the beauty and splendor of the city. The masonic fraternity is also erecting a most handsome and gigantic temple which promises to be an ornament to Palestine and would indeed be a pride to any city.

Our Israelitish brethren are also aiding liberally in building up the city, and a great many of them are real estate owners, and those that suffered by the late fire are now replacing their old wooden buildings by fine brick store-houses, two stories high. All seems to be in glee and full of good prospects, satisfied with true Palestine, and are not willing any longer to repeat the prayer of the Hagadah,[71] that next year they may be in the true Palestine. I remonstrated with them arguing that they are committing a crime and a sin if they omit this most sacred prayer.[72] Yet we could not convince them otherwise, and we were much surprised to find that there are Jews in America who do not pray for the return to Palestine, and much more that they decline to go even if they could. Alas, after due reflection we thought that they may be correct in their views after all and that this land of liberty and freedom, this State of fertile soil and

---

[71] *Haggadah* (pronounced ha-gah-dah) means "narrative" or "telling." It is a set form of benedictions, prayers, psalms, and stories recited at the *seder* (see note 16 above), the ritual dinner during the Jewish celebration of the Passover, which centers around the retelling of, and moralizing about, the exodus of the Jews from Egypt. Passover is a holiday which celebrates the joys of freedom, and frequently was personalized by the immigrants who equated Egypt with their homelands in Europe or elsewhere, and the United States with the land of milk and honey. (During the days of the Roman Empire the holiday took on special meaning. It became one of the most important holidays as it is today.)

[72] With the destruction of the Temple, the *seder* (pronounced say-dah, and meaning "order of service") received greater emphasis and the *Haggadah* was furnished with language of symbolic meaning and the *seder* became a home service. Among the focal prayers, the one that emphasized the idea of liberty, of inner moral and spiritual liberty, was the *Ha lahma*, "Behold!" This prayer is often interpreted in a Zionist vein of a desire to return to Palestine, for it reads "At present, we celebrate it (Passover) here, may we celebrate it next year in the land of Israel." The Reform Movement generally rejected the meaning of this passage arguing, as Wessolowsky indicates in his letter, that it was not to be taken literally but merely as a symbolic statement for the quest of freedom which was attained in the United States.

rich prairies, with all of its facilities and advantages may perhaps be preferable and more sought for than the dry and barren country of the Palestine of our fathers. Thus we concluded that we are also willing to remain in this country and will use next year, one of those abridged hagadahs, which is filled up simply with prayers over matzos, eggs, and saltwater, etc.[73]

Our Israelites here number about one hundred souls and eleven Jewish families; every one engaged in business, perfectly enwrapped in it, so that everything else is forgotten, neglected and considered a secondary item—no Sunday School, no ladies' society, nothing that perhaps could stimulate them and further the ends of sociability— or would make them feel that they are Israelites and that a duty is encumbered upon them as parents to teach their children.

We were pleased to meet Mr. and Mrs. Muskowitz, and received the promise of the latter that she with the aid of other ladies will endeavor to inaugurate some ladies' societies and thereby try to promote harmonious feeling among our people in Palestine.

After remaining here two days we took the train for Hearn, where we had to tarry for about twelve hours with our brethren and soon departed for Calvert. Here we met Dr. Epstein and Mr. Sayard, and became their guest.

Calvert has indeed lately played such a conspicuous part in the columns of the *Jewish South* that no doubt all of its readers are acquainted with the location, situation and everything appertaining to Jewish matters, judging it from the stand point as "F," in his article endeavors to describe, but as an impartial judge, one who has no further interest than simply to give facts as they truly exist. We thought that perhaps a few words from us would shed some light

---

[73]These items refer to the ceremonial items used during the Passover celebration at the *seder*. The *matzos* is eaten in memory of the "bread of affliction" prepared by the Israelites during their hasty flight from Egypt. The egg, which is roasted, stands for the festival offering at the time of the Temple. Saltwater is used in which was dipped parsley as an added festivity, for it was considered a delicacy in ancient times. Other rituals include a shoulder bone representing the pascal lamb; bitter herbs, usually horseradish, for the bitter plight of the Jews in slavery; and *harosis* or *haroseth* (pronounced har-ros-ease), a delicious mixture of ground nuts, apples, cinnamon and red wine, to symbolize the clay with which Jews worked to make bricks for the pharohs.

upon the controversy appearing in the *Jewish South* between "F," "Leon Strauss" and "Harmony."[74]

We remained here several days, had occasion to examine into everything that perhaps could give us opportunities to ascertain whether the statements made by "F" are coupled with facts and written in the spirit of candor and truth, or whether the gentleman permitted his maliced spirit of revenge, or any other dark hidden motive to prompt him in penning the article to which he signed himself "F.," and I must candidly say, in the name of our motto, "Independent and fearless," that "F." has overstepped widely the boundaries of truth, and that with the exception, "that Calvert is the county seat of Robertson county," his article contains nothing but misstatements, made no doubt either by being misinformed, or his being harsh and partial judge. His charges were denied in full by Mr. Strauss, a gentleman who for the sake of learning an honorable livelihood, has assumed the position as teacher and instructor of the Jewish children in Calvert, and how he succeeds and what progress the children have made under his administration, can only be judged by gentlemen who have any knowledge of the branches he teaches and who feel that they ought not to pass their judgement, without previously making examination and inquiries into it. We did so; we visited the school of Mr. Strauss and found about twenty children from six to ten years old, well behaved, well disciplined, advanced not alone in their English and other branches but we actually heard children of six years of age reading Hebrew fluently and able to translate some, and all this taught in the course of six months. This is the work of one old fogey as "F" will style the gentleman, this is the labor of the "northern importation." Would to heaven, that we had many such old fogies, many who could make their life as useful as this Mr. Strauss does and less "Fs" in this world, who are only obstruction and obstacles in the smooth path of such an honorable life and as that which Mr. Strauss is leading. But we trust that no such articles will weaken the courage and zeal of Mr. Strauss and that he will continue in his ardent duties and succeed in the future as well as he did in the branches he now teaches and which our readers will fully agree with us, when they read

---

[74]See *Jewish South*, March-April 1879, *passim*.

articles written by the gentleman for the *Jewish South*. We sympathize with Mr. Strauss and with the Yehudim [Hebrews] in general in Calvert, to be slandered in any such unjust and untruthful manner.

We remained here over Sunday, made many acquaintances, and we trust friends, and upon invitation we lectured at the Opera House. Our time was pleasantly spent, and we are indebted to two young ladies for the sight of a beautiful lake to which our promenade led us, a little description of the so commonly called "Lake of Lovers Petocal," may be interesting to some who may peruse this.

This lake is about one mile from Calvert, covering an area of about one hundred and fifty acres. Nature has placed a charming lake to dazzle the eye of the beholder, and make happy the heart of every living thing in its vicinity, particularly those who visit this lover's retreat. The scenery around it is very romantic, its many natural curiosities affording ample pleasure and study for all lovers of the beautiful. The lake with its bluffs stretching into its crystal waters affords good fishing, boating and duck shooting. There are two beautiful houses nearby for the pleasure of visitors and have the capacity of accommodating two hundred guests, all facilities for amusement, sport, fun, are liberally supplied and we may truly call it a place of pleasure, health and recreation. Those who long to leave the noisy streets of Calvert, and rush of business when heat and headache hold their matinees, may go to that romantic spot where our heart and spirit hold communion with murmuring waters, forests, birds and flowers. We were indeed charmed with the scene, and will ever remember how beautiful and delightful, all this in imagination, when in reality we behold a pond with an old wooden shanty near it, which is called "The Lovers Retreat."

To our friends who so kindly treated us during our stay in Calvert we return thanks and we shall ever be pleased to meet them.

We left Calvert for Marlin. More in our next.

C. W.

Letter Number Fifteen

Charles Wessolowsky to Rabbi Edward B. M. Browne

Marlin, Waco, and
Corsicana, Texas
May 1879

• • •

[*In Marlin, Texas, where eight Jewish families live,
Wessolowsky meets the learned Mr. Malevin; he describes both
the commercial and residential districts of Waco, Texas, in
which work and live thirty Jewish families, economically
successful and religiously active; he advocates the
establishment of a ladies' aid society; he spent Shevuos in
Corsicana, Texas, but no holiday services took place; there are
twelve Jewish families living there that do not practice their
religion even though they have formed a B'nai B'rith Lodge.*]

• • •

At Marlin, a place of about two thousand inhabitants and
situated on a branch of the H. &. T. Central Road, will be found
about eight Jewish families and perhaps fifty Jewish souls. We were
nicely entertained by them being the guest of Mr. Philiposki,
partner of the firm Levy Rosenthal & Philiposki, who are doing a
very extensive business. Here we met a Mr. Malevin and whom we
regard as the "walking Talmud," and indeed his knowledge in all
Hebrew branches startled us as his memory and recollection in all
parts of the Talmud and other works seems to be as fresh as if he just
would have left the Jesheweh,[75] while the gentleman is many years in
this country and engaged in mercantile pursuits; we spent six hours
in his company and will ever remember the pleasing event.

We remained here overnight, enjoyed the hospitalities of our
host and hostess, and in company of Mr. S. Samuels, the bold
cotton buyer, returned to Calvert and took the train to Waco.

---

[75]Sometimes *yeshiva* (pronounced yeh-shee-vah). The *yeshiva* is a talmudic
academy first founded in Lithuania in the 17th century. The appearance of the
yeshiva marked the beginning of an intellectual movement among Russian Jewry
sometimes called the "Vilna School."

We arrived here in the evening, became the guest of Mr. and Mrs. Sam Sanger, whom we have met in Calvert, and there accepted his invitation.

This city named after an Indian tribe, is one that may be numbered among the beautiful cities of Texas.

Her large commercial houses and the energy and enterprise of her people, the perseverance and exertions of all within her have been noted by all who visit Waco and all are a unit in bespeaking for Waco a great and prosperous future and the remarks are general that Waco is destined to become a large and extensive commercial city. We were much pleased with its appearance and were indeed surprised to find so many improvements of various kinds, that are adorning and beautifying the city, all of which are the work and accomplishment of but a few late years. Handsome business houses, extensive establishments in the latest and modern style, most tastefully arranged, and in every respect equal to any Northern business, are the most attractive features of the city. The handsome private residences with their beautiful and fragrant flower gardens in front, the most elegant public structures and edifices with improvements of the latest patterns, greets the eye of the stranger in every direction, and he is forced to recognize the fact that Waco is a charming and handsome city.

Our Israelitish brethren here numbering about two hundred souls and perhaps about thirty families, are not less energetic in the accomplishments of all for Waco, and some of them are indeed front in rank in every branch of industry and commerce. They exhibit here their thrift, their zeal, and enterprising spirits, as well as elsewhere; and the fertile mind of the Jew is also brought here in requisition for the welfare and prosperity of the city. Such business houses as those of Lessing, Lyons, Solomon & Co., of which firm, our friend, Mr. Meyer late from Pensacola, is now a partner, are indeed but very few in the State; and in point of taste, elegance, style, and beauty, equal to any North or West. This mammoth establishment, and that of Messrs. Gauger Bros., adds greatly to the attraction and beauty of the city, and brings no doubt a great many strangers to Waco to purchase their goods, who otherwise perhaps would seek another channel.

There are also other large business houses carried on by our brethren, yet not on such an extensive scale as the above named, and we were proud to find them here, also enjoying a high standing and a good reputation as strict and reliable businessmen and gentlemen of integrity and honesty.

They are also large property holders and have as far as we could ascertain, the handsomest buildings in the city.

The storehouse of Messrs. Lyons, Solomon & Co., is indeed grand and a pride to any city, and the private residence of Messrs. Alexander, Solomon, Sanger, Lewine, Lyons, and others too numerous to mention, are numbered among the most elegant and costly structures within the city.

We were also pleased to find that our brothers here are not indifferent to the cause of Judaism. They have a Eureka I. O. B. B. Lodge, with C. Lachman as President; B. Ettelson, Vice-President; and Chas. Beer, Secretary, and it is in good working order.

Also, a congregation "Rodeph Sholem,"[76] with Mr. S. Sanger as President, and the question is now strongly agitated, and I trust with good result, whether to build a temple or not. We feel satisfied, that our brothers in Waco are well able and willing to imitate the good example set them by our brothers in Dallas and elsewhere, and that before long, with their usual energy and zeal, will exhibit the same in this particular and erect an edifice signifying their practical work, and that they are indeed, a people who are "Rodelph Sholem" seeking peace and union.

There also exists here a Hebrew Benevolent Society, with Mr. Alexander as president. The Society is bestowing aid to all needy and is performing general good through its noble deeds.

Upon request, we lectured at the courthouse to a large audience of Jews and Gentiles; also on Sunday afternoon, principally to Israelites, upon the subject of B'nai B'rith and the erection of a synagogue. We flatter ourselves that our words have found room in their hearts, and that we will behold the fruits of our labor in the existence of a nice and neat temple, worthy of the name and reputation of the Israelites of Waco.

Our Jewish ladies here have as yet no society, and with your permission we desire to say to you, that upon you depends the success of this undertaking of building the synagogue. You with

---

[76]*Rodeph Sholom* (pronounced ro-def sha-lam) means "Pursuing peace."

your persuasive powers, zeal and enthusiasm for the cause, can indeed bring into its ranks many who are now indifferent and entirely careless about it. You can fan into life the long smothered flame, and bring it to seek a headway that to check it would be impossible. Upon you mothers in Israel devolves this duty, and if you, with your earnestness and devotion will enlist your energy in behalf of the cause, who can and who will doubt its result? We may surely count upon its final achievement, and how proud would each mother of you feel, when you can with a finger of pride point to your offspring, the works of your hands. Begin the noble work and may we have the pleasure soon to record in our columns, the success and good results which naturally must crown your efforts.

We were pleased to meet Mr. Lehman Sanger, whom we knew twenty-one years ago, and who honored us with his presence at our engagement. To Mr. and Mrs. L. Sanger, who spared no trouble to make us feel at home in their house, we return our best thanks, also to Messrs. Lewine, Solomon, Friedlander and others, who so kindly favored us.

Monday morning we bade adieu to all and started across the bridge to take the train, but to our astonishment we learned that the *transfer company* neglected to bring our trunk. We felt of course disappointed and wished that the transfer company would transfer their business to some one who would transfer baggage without their hope of being transferred into disppointment and so naturally saying "Gam so Letovah" [out of bad comes some good], we returned to the city and spent a most agreeable day, visited several of our friends and in the evening took courage to be transferred by the same company to East Waco, where we took the train for Corsicana, and arrived there the following afternoon. Here we spent our Shevuos, the Feast of Weeks, but not in such a manner and place as we would desire, as there is no temple here, and consequently we were deprived of witnessing the beautiful confirmation ceremony. We made ourselves satisfied spending the day in getting acquainted with our brothers, whom we found to be pleasant and agreeable.

Among the 4,000 inhabitants of this city, there are about twelve Jewish families. Here again, we found that the youth are neglected and that the command, "Thou shall teach it diligently to thy children,"[77] is entirely forgotten. The Sunday School established some time ago by Rev. Mr. Blum, of Galveston is out of date, no pupils and no teacher to be found, no one cares and thus it rocks along to the injury and neglect of the Jewish children. We took occasion to speak to some of the ladies in its behalf and in our lecture in the B. B. Lodge made mention that it is one of the teachings and purposes of the order. We hope that ere long, parents in Corsicana will awaken to their duty and let their children at least receive the necessary instruction in the Jewish religion. Otherwise our Israelitish brethren here seem to be prosperous, and are carrying on extensive business.

The B. B. Lodge with Bro. Deutschner as President is now in very good condition and full of life and debate.

We remained here two days, spent our time pleasantly and left Corsicana enroute for Dallas.

C. W.

P.S. We notice that we have omitted to say that we stopped in Mexia before we reached Corsicana if our brothers will pardon us, we promise them to do so in our next, and never again to be guilty of such an oversight.

C. W.

---

[77]This passage is part of the *Shema Israel* from Deut. 6:4-9, which enjoined the teaching of the basic dogma and duty of Judaism, that is, the law. The commands were to keep the law constantly in the forefront of a person's mind: he was to recite the Love of and Unity of God when he woke up and when he went to sleep; he was to constantly discuss them even as he "walking by the way"; they were to be signs (*mezuzah*) on doors and on gates; they were to be taught to and passed on to the coming generation; and they were to be signs on hands and forehead—a precept fulfilled by the wearing of phylacteries.

Letter Number Sixteen

Charles Wessolowsky to Rabbi Edward B. M. Browne

Mexia, Ennis, and
Dallas, Texas
May 1879

• • •

[*Wessolowsky notes that six Jewish families live in Mexia and another ten in Ennis; but the majority of the letter is devoted to the seventy Jewish families living in Dallas; he describes the department store of Sanger Bros.; he then goes on to discuss the religious activities of the Jewish community as well as its active involvement in the social life of Dallas.*]

• • •

We reached Mexia from Waco and remained over until our next train. Here we found about six Jewish families, all very much respected and honored. They follow the usual avocation and are doing well.

Mr. Weiss had been extremely kind to us, and we were pleased with the Israelites of Mexia, who seem to be courteous and clever.

In the afternoon we left for Corsicana, (of which we wrote in our last) and from there on our route for Dallas we stopped at Ennis, a small place of about fifteen hundred inhabitants, with about fifty souls; here we met Mr. Lyons, of Waco, who interested himself in our behalf, and in the afternoon we took the train for Dallas, where we arrived Friday evening.

This metropolis of the northern part of Texas, with her gigantic structures, mammoth and extensive business houses, grand and spacious establishments, elegant and beautiful residences, large and commodious hotels, is to the stranger, of great attraction and admiration. Here he is in the midst of gaiety and pleasure, enjoyment and life, ease and comfort, and he is soon made to feel that Dallas, with her proverbial hospitality so lavishly bestowed upon every worthy stranger, merits fully the good name and reputation she bears, and her citizens are indeed deserving the laudatory praises, which are uttered by nearly every stranger who visits the place.

Here he also finds a city with all modern improvements, her citizens thrifty and energetic people, wide-awake and with exceptionable enterprise, beautifying and adorning the city and extending their might, energy and perseverance for the speedy development and growth of their material interest, and are in every respect using their efforts and zeal to make Dallas the Venice of Texas. And with the knowledge that in the lexicon of the leading enterprises of the day there is "no such word as fail," we feel assured that all undertakings of Dallas, will be of great utility, beauty and profit, and without giving rein to imagination it is not too much to say, that the future will make it equal in size, splendor and beauty to any interior city in the state.

Dallas numbers about 20,000 inhabitants, among them we find about 500 Jewish souls and about seventy Jewish families.

Our Israelites here, in their various avocations and stations of life, are aiding vastly in bringing about the desired success for Dallas and some of them are enjoying the reputation and fame of doing the largest and most extensive business in the city.

We enter the business house of Sanger Bros.,[78] and we at once perceive and behold an establishment of grandeur, taste and elegance, equal to any in the South, and so systematically and well arranged, that in the opinion of some travelers it surpasses any business North. The lower floor wherein retail customers, even those of the most fastidious taste are served about thirty clerks, male and female, is 200 feet long, containing everything that may be asked, or called for in a business of this kind, and is visited daily by a throng of people, so that in entering the same, a person imagines himself to be in Stuart's establishment in the city of New York.[79] The upper floors are used exclusively for wholesale and filled with merchandise of all kinds and descriptions, to meet the demands of all their customers, which by the integrity, honesty and square dealing of employer and employees have become very numerous.

There are also magnificent and mammoth establishments kept by our co-religionists, which are all a credit and honor to any city.

---

[78]For a history of this great Texas "emporium" see Leon Rosenberg, *Sangers: Pioneer Texas Merchants* (Austin, Texas: Texas Historical Association, 1978).

[79]See Robert Henrickson, *The Grand Emporiums* (New York: Stein & Day, 1978).

We must forgo the pleasure of mentioning them in detail, as time and space will not permit it. Our brothers here are enjoying the respect and friendship of the Gentile community and are participating largely in every measure, that is tending toward advancing the welfare of the city.

We were pleased to meet Mr. Phillip Sanger, whom we used to know in Georgia and to find him in connection with his brothers in a position of fame and prosperity, also to shake hands with the veteran or as many call him the "Old War Horse," Bro. D. Goslin and also our countryman Mr. Wolf and Dr. Tillman, all three we had the pleasure of meeting at the Grand Lodge session in New Orleans.

We were also glad to see that our brothers here are displaying a great interest in the cause of Judaism, and thus we find a flourishing Dallas I. O. B. B. Lodge, with Bro. J. E. Wolf as President, and with a membership of sixty-one, also Lone Star K. S. B. [Kesher Shel Barzel] Lodge, with Bro. Alex Sanger as President, in very good working order, and has thirty-five members.

A. H. B. Association, Dr. E. M. Tillman, President—the institution being the oldest in the city may be properly called the mother institution; it is doing a vast deal of good, dispensing charity to all who call upon its coffers.

We also find Emmanuel Lodge Congregation with Mr. David Goslin as president, and Rev. A. Suhler as its spiritual guide in very thriving condition. This Rev. Mr. Suhler is a polished and learned gentleman, who labors and toils for the cause of Judaism and has occupied the function as rabbi of the congregation in Dallas for the past four years. We attended services in the gorgeous and handsome temple and listened to sweet and excellent music produced by the choir, which is composed of the following ladies and gentlemen: Mrs. L. Goslin, Misses Oppenheimer and Goldsmith and Mr. Friedberger. All of them taking delight in the performance of their duties, and very punctual in their attendance.

It gives us also pleasure to chronicle that our Jewish ladies of Dallas are contributing their share of love's labor as well, and that a L. H. B. Association is aiding and assisting the cause of Judaism and is in very prosperous circumstances. Its officers are as follows: Mrs. Metzler, President; Mrs. Goldsmith, Vice-President; Mrs. Baum, Trustee; Mrs. S. C. Rosenthal, Secretary.

By invitation of some of our brothers, we entered the Senate Chamber, corner Main Street, and were pleased to see so many of our co-religionists elevated to various high positions. Thus we found Bro. Goslin as President of the Senate, presiding with his usual dignity, giving honor to the function, and never at a loss how to decide a parliamentary question. Bro. S. Loeb, Secretary of the Senate, acting at the same time as Reading Clerk, ever ready to aid and assist the president in his labor, is indeed the right man in the right place and we were delighted to hear his clear, ringing and distinct voice at the reading of bills, which makes it very intelligible to the members present. Mr. Metzler, in his capacity as journalizing clerk, and Dr. Tillman as chairman of the Enrolling Committee are very industrious in the performance of their respective duties, and are indeed an ornament to any Senate chamber, Bro. J. E. Wolf as chairman of the Judiciary Committee, is ever prepared with his eloquence and logical arguments, to defend all recommendations made by the committee, and he is indeed a bright, shining light in the legal fraternity, and his power is felt vastly in the Senate chamber. Mr. Aaron Marks, the owner of the chamber, is the janitor of the Senate, who, of course, at the bidding of the Senators, provides them with all necessary accommodations, and is so attentive and courteous to them that his re-election as janitor is most certain. Others, in their duties as Senators are very attentive, listening to the various bills, particularly those of the local option law, and unanimous in their votes and electioneering, are defeating every measure that is brought before them, tending to that effect, as they believe, in this land of freedom, no restriction of any sort, even as to the sale of any kind of beverage should be imposed upon any citizen. Thus we spent several hours in the Senate chamber, listening intentively and indulging in some remarks ourselves whenever called upon, and were indeed pleased and delighted to have an opportunity of spending our time in such good and agreeable company.

Mr. A. Z. Rosenthal, the polite and affable gentleman, superintendent of the wholesale department of Sanger Bros., has placed us under many obligations.

We visited also the Sunday School, conducted by Rev. A. Suhler and aided by many ladies and gentlemen, whose names we do not now remember and trust that our contributor from Dallas will name them in his next letter. We found the scholars proficient in their studies, and upon request we addressed the children, and also gave a public lecture to a large audience in the synagogue.

We were also pleased to meet Mr. and Mrs. A. Sanger, who but lately have been united into wedlock. We wish them a safe voyage upon their matrimonial sea.

To all ladies and gentlemen who have made our stay so pleasant in the city of Dallas, we return our thanks and ever shall cherish in our memory the delightful time spent among them.

Tuesday evening we left for Fort Worth and promised to return to Waco on Thursday.

C. W.

P.S. The Senate Chamber above alluded to is a celebrated coffee house in the city of Dallas. Mr. Aaron Marks, the accommodating and polite gentleman, is the proprietor. By his strict attention to the wants of his customers, the place became famous and is now one of the finest in Texas, which of course our co-religionists visit.

C. W.

Letter Number Seventeen

Charles Wessolowsky to Rabbi Edward B. M. Browne

Fort Worth, Sherman,
Dennison, and Paris, Texas
June 1879

● ● ●

[*Wessolowsky talks of twelve families in Fort Worth and reprimands the parents for their laxity in teaching their children in the ways of Judaism; twenty families live in Sherman who are well-to-do but religiously inactive; Dennison boasts of ten Jewish families as does Paris.*]

● ● ●

We reached Fort Worth in due time, started out to meet our brothers, whom we found to be about one hundred in number, and perhaps about twelve Jewish families. All are industrious, hardworking and energetic people. This is somewhat of a frontier place and does a good deal of business with those residing immediately on the Mexican frontier, and all there seemed to be doing well. There is an I. O. B. B. Lodge with Bro. S. L. Turk as President, and a Hebrew Educational and Charitable Society, Isaac Cohen, President. Both are seemingly now in good working order, and thriving circumstances.

Some time ago, Rev. A. Blum, of Galveston, instituted a Sunday School at this place, with Joseph Meyer as Principal, and Misses Julia and Rosa Weiner and Dora Fry, as teachers, We could not visit the school, but from inquiries, found that the teachers are performing their duties faithfully; the children are progressing, but there seems to be a lack of zeal among parents, who are not very much disposed to take great interest in the education of their children in that branch of moral and religious teaching. Why is this? From nearly every section of the country the pleasing news is heralded that the Jewish children are of the brightest wits, the best scholars in the public schools, and the reason for the same is given that besides their inherent quickness of intellect, parents in their home government watch of their progress in study and learning and exhibit a greater desire and zeal for the promotion of their children, and also use all their efforts to sustain the recommendation of their teachers and to furnish them with everything necessary and whatever is required, and keep themselves posted and advised of the progress of their children. Then we ask again why is it that Jewish parents of Fort Worth do not demonstrate that enthusiasm, and pursue with earnestness and order the object which they as parents are responsible to them, aye to God and all mankind? We trust that this will give food for reflection and that hereafter the indifference existing (no doubt for some cause) will be dispelled, and enthusiasm and zeal substituted. We trust that we have not wounded the feelings of any one and are only discharging our duty which is encumbered upon us.

We spent two days very agreeably in the city, and our brothers have done all in their power to make us feel at home for which we are very grateful.

We left Fort Worth for Dallas, and from there took the trains for Sherman, where we arrived Sunday noon and soon found ourselves in company of Bro. Van Ronkle, who was extremely kind to us.

Here we formed the acquaintance of Maj. Levy, the well known vindicator of Judaism, who has so often by his able pen, learned and logical arguments, clear and distinct reasons, hurled back the slander and defamation and false accusation brought against Jews and Judaism by some narrow-minded and bigoted man or men, and who by his talented learning, and the bold and open defense against the attacks and criticism made upon the lecture of crucifixion delivered by Dr. Browne,[80] has merited the honor and respect he so justly deserves—we were proud to meet him and be thankful to him for courtesies shown to us.

---

[80]Browne was always under attack by both Jew and Gentile for venturing into "forbidden waters." Isaac Wise and Browne, for example, never did agree on the propriety of publishing a regional Jewish newspaper that at the same time catered to the Gentile population. On the other hand, Browne argued that by informing the Gentiles of Jewish ways and activities an understanding of the Jews and respect for their ways could be created. In this way prospective prejudice could be minimized. At the same time, many Gentile clergymen though it was contemptuous that a Jew should speak about the crucifixion and resurrection in a rationalistic-moralistic manner. While Browne's speech has not been found, indications of these running disputes are found throughout the *Jewish South*.

Sherman is located on the Texas Central R. R., and has a population of about ten thousand inhabitants, among whom we find about twenty Jewish families and perhaps about one hundred Jewish souls. The most extensive and largest business is done by Messrs. Schneider & Co., and co-religionists, who have a most elegant and beautiful business place, tastefully and splendidly arranged, and are doing well. There are many other large business houses carried on by brothers and all seem to progress fairly. A B. B. Lodge with Bro. Hernstadt as president is doing well here, full of life and debate.

We regret that we cannot record any other Jewish institution, nor even a regular Sunday School, and we most respectfully ask our readers in Sherman to peruse carefully our remarks made above.

Bro. Wm. Van Ronkle has placed us under many obligations and we return our thanks to him and to his most interesting family.

We are pleased to meet Mr. Ripynaki, and to see him do well.

Tuesday, bidding adieu to our friends, we started for Dennison, the terminus of that great and safe Texas C. R. R.

We landed at night and soon in the morning were aroused by loud "hurrahs" of a joyful multitude of people, who in their expression of satisfaction and pleasure gave vent to their feeling and rent the air with shouts of joy and exaltation. We were amazed, astonished and wondered the cause of all this. We soon were told that they are the visitors in a municipal election which was held a day previous, and it together with a picnic on some near place on the railroad, brought all those people out who now feel that they have saved the country from all further evil and corruption, for reason that their man was elected mayor of the city of Dennison. We had no direct interest in this election yet we felt joyful to know that we are living in this great land of freedom where the voices of the people select their rulers and where all can exercise the free right of citizenship and with his ballot elect or reject him, who may or may not be his choice.

We met Dr. Hernstadt, from Sherman, who introduced us to our brothers. We found perhaps ten Jewish families, all engaged in mercantile business, and getting along.

Our friend Herman Kuhn the local editor of a daily paper (name unknown to us) [Dennison *Evening Herald*], was very kind to us, and we are pleased to see the gentleman in a position which is elevating to Judaism.

Sorry that we cannot record here anything appertaining to Jewish matters. That afternoon we left Dennison and went back to Sherman and from thence started for Paris, and reached there Thursday night. Here we beheld a handsome little city of about five thousand inhabitants and about ten Jewish families. We found good society, schools, churches and other institutions, which build up a community. Our Jewish population is aiding vastly in making Paris a city, in every sense of the word.

We were pleased to meet Mr. Tobias Cohen, and who kindly introduced us to Miss Freese, in whose company we spent a delightful evening, listening to her excellent and charming music, until we were reminded that it was train time and must depart.

Taking leave of our friends we left Paris for Texarkana.

C. W.

Letter Number Eighteen

Charles Wessolowsky to Rabbi Edward B. M. Browne

Texarkana, Jefferson, and
Marshall, Texas
June 1879

• • •

[*Wessolowsky notes that there are ten Jewish families living in Texarkana without any religious activity and displaying assimilationist tendencies; the twenty Jewish families in Jefferson, Texas, are carrying on large businesses and hold public office; he contrasts this Jewish community's activity with those communities he just visited; he talks of a B'nai B'rith Lodge in Marshall that is supported by that town's twelve Jewish families—end of Texas tour.*]

• • •

Texarkana, a city of a few thousand inhabitants, of which a portion is in the State of Texas, the other in Arkansas, and therefore the name of TEX-ARK-ANA, is a place of some notoriety, on account of being the great railroad center and connecting line between Texas, St. Louis and Memphis.

Here we met Messrs. A. Borg and Meyer, of Hope, Ark., whose acquaintance we were pleased to form, and also General Nobles the polite and efficient Superintendent of the Texas and Pacific Railroad, who indeed bestowed many courtesies upon us.

We found here, about ten Jewish families and perhaps seventy-five souls, but without any Jewish organization or anything that has the tendency to make them remember, that they are followers of Judaism except perhaps on our most important holidays (in their opinion) they endeavor to have worship, and at times an apostate Jew, now being a staunch Christian (no doubt for some hidden motive, like Rosevalley, Jaeger, Reider & Co.,) is the selected preacher. He like others of his kind with continual practice of hypocrisy, without sincerity and with false pretenses, sailing under the colors of assumed Christian piety while in fact they are neither Jews nor Christians, like a snake they try to charm others with their smooth venomous tongue expressing their little knowledge of our religion, or of the sayings of our sages, sometimes in the camp of

Israel (if Jews forget themselves) and at other times before Christian audiences; yet, it has no weight as their true principles and the mercenary motives are known and their words fall like chaff before the wind. But we hope that for the sake of Judaism and Christianity, as he who is, pure true and strictly following the precepts of Jesus can only be a Christian, such hypocrites with their deceptive countenances and appearance will never be permitted either in the synagogue or church, to mislead others, and to carry out their hidden selfish motives and their own personal interests.

We remained here until next morning, when we took the train for Jefferson, and arrived there Friday noon.

We were struck with the buildings that we saw, large cotton warehouses and immense brick stores, elegant private residences, which were more or less in a state of decay, and a great many of them unoccupied, yet showing distinctly that Jefferson was once a large commercial city; and has contributed vastly to the prosperity of Texas.

But while Jefferson has lost some of her grandeur and greatness, yet she may be numbered among the active and thriving cities of the state. With a population of about five thousand, she still boasts today of mammoth and extensive business houses, and majestically and defiantly asking where is the greater? She is still the commercial outlet for merchants of hundreds of miles around her, and the reservoir from which many draw their necessary supplies of food, clothing and farming utensils.

Our Israelitish brethren here, whom we found to number about one hundred and fifty souls and about twenty families, are carrying on the largest business in the place. The wholesale house of K. Mendel & Co., with their large and extensive stock of merchandise kept in various warehouses, consisting of all kinds that may be wanted or needed in their section of the country is doing business by the millions and is indeed a pride and honor to any city, and we may safely say that but very few are its equal. This and many other large houses carried on by our brothers, too numerous to mention, exhibit clearly to the stranger that here our brothers have the entire control of the mercantile business and no doubt, like anywhere else is a prospective feature for good. But it is not alone in the mercantile world that they are great, but even in the eyes of our President Hayes, a noble Jewish lady worthy of being the mother of "Easter" is made Postmistress, which office we understand her husband in lifetime held and she now is holding for years to the great satisfaction and gratification of all. We were pleased to meet a Jewish lady with the fact of doing business, which she has, being one of the United States officers, and although we are not one of the admirers of Mr. Hayes, neither of his official acts, yet we tip our hat to his Excellency for the appointment of such a worthy lady as Mrs. Sterne, to the office as postmistress, and consider it a wise and prudent act of our famous Rutherford B. Hayes, and perhaps the wisest in his official career.

But while this is singularizing and speaking of individuals, we have a greater encomium to bestow upon our brothers in Jefferson, more laudatory praises than merely eulogizing them for their mercantile capacity. It is for the blessing of "Union and Harmony," which prevails among them—it is for the liberal tolerant spirit, and brotherly feeling, which they possess. They are the living statues, towering toward heaven, which ornament and extol the Israelites of Jefferson, they truly represent the brotherhood of Israel. Here we find no distinction of nationality, no preference of wealth, no regard for station, but all are impressed with that teaching "like unto me, my fellow man is a child of God." We were highly pleased with our brothers here, and may their example of peace and union be imitated by many of our co-religionists at other places.

We met with pleasure our old friend Mr. Eberstadt and by the courtesy of his amiable lady, we had an opportunity of witnessing the rehearsal of the opera "Esther, the beautiful Queen," although many of the important characters were not present, yet the singing and performance of the drama, the acting of the cast and the excellent music on the piano, all were rendered in such a mode and manner, that to me it was an evening of leisure, and we were loud in our expression of admiration, for a cast composed only of amateurs, and who well deserve the name of professionals. We would like to speak in detail upon the merits and qualifications of each actor, but our space will not permit it, and when we mention the great credit is due to Mrs. W. H. Mason, as musical directress, and Mrs. E. Eberstadt, as pianist, whose skill and talent on the piano is famous, we do not wish to pluck any of the laurels all others so justly deserve. Esther, the daughter of our worthy postmistress, Mrs. Eva Sterne, how right is she entitled to the epitaph of "beautiful queen," lovely handsome, and beautiful as she is, she presented the simplicity of the great queen, pleading for the safety of her people, with her melodious, sweet and captivating voice, that we wished to have been the King Ahasuerus, to have the opportunity of granting her requests. We were deprived of witnessing the performance on June 19th, and hope that their labors were rewarded by a liberal patronage of the citizens of Jefferson.[81]

Our Israelites here have a handsome temple and a beautiful parsonage; but for the present no minister. We trust that ere long they will boast of some good pulpit orator who will expound the doctrines of Judaism, before Jew and Gentiles. The congregation, with E. Eberstadt as president, is in flourishing condition.

Our friends, Max Munzerheimer, the affable and kind gentleman has placed us under many obligations, and we return thanks for courtesies; also, to Messrs. Corey, Repyeski and others.

We will ever cherish in memory, our pleasant stay in the city, the kind and generous treatment we received at the hands of all our brothers, and will forever treasure up the parables and wholesome teachings of our witty brother, Mr. Goldberg.

We remained here until Monday noon, when we started in company with Mr. Munzerheimer, for Marshall, where we arrived about 3 o'clock p.m.

Marshall, the terminus of the T. and P. R. R. presents a nice appearance and has about 8000 inhabitants, and about twelve Jewish families.

There is an I. O. B. B. Lodge here with Joe Wiseman as president, and as we learned is getting along well.

Here we remained until next morning when we started for Shreveport, La. This ended our Texas tour and in bidding adieu to all our brothers and friends in the "Lone Star State" we again express our heartfelt thanks for all the kindness and attention we received from them, and while we perhaps, in our letters were forced to give a more extensive description of some places than others, and again by force of circumstances were necessitated to speak more

---

[81]King Ahasuerus was the Persian king found in the story of the Book of Esther to whom Esther was consort, and who saved the Jews from the plots of his chief adviser, Haman.

truth than fiction, believe us brethren, one and all, it is done in a friendly and brotherly spirit and with malice to none. In discharging our duty it became necessary that the picture required more true and unfading colors, and we simply laid on the brush upon the stretched canvas to portray it according as we thought was necessary for the elevation and advancement of the cause of Judaism. Again we thank you and hope that we will soon meet again.

C. W.

P.S. We omitted to state that Jefferson has also a Hebrew B. Society, with U. P. Levy as president, and is doing a vast deal of good.

C. W.

Letter Number Nineteen

Charles Wessolowsky to Rabbi Edward B. M. Browne

Shreveport and
Alexandria, Louisiana
July 1879

• • •

[*In Shreveport, Wessolowsky identifies the rabbi who officiated there as spiritual head of the Congregation Hebrew Zion; he notes that the activities of the temple are supported by a variety of men's and ladies' societies; and among the population of Alexandria are 150 Jews many of whom hold high political office in the city; and he describes Friday night service at the temple, the Sunday School, and the various charitable organizations; then he returned to New Orleans.*]

• • •

The Texas and Pacific Railroad landed us safely upon Louisiana soil, and we reached Shreveport Tuesday noon. After having shaken the dust from us, we proceeded at once to look for our old friend Wm. Winter. We found him in full bloom of life, enjoying the good will and wishes of all who know him; and although being Winter, complaining severely of the hot weather. Bro. Winter soon introduced us to many of our co-religionists and most prominent among them was the Rev. Dr. Greenblatt, who is here on a visit with his family, and whom we were delighted to meet. The reverend gentleman was minister of Shreveport congregation for five years and is now in Pine Bluff, Ark., where he is working zealously and faithfully for the cause of Judaism, and with his eloquence and most excellent sermons and lectures is elevating it in the eyes of the Gentiles, and is justly deserving the praise and credit bestowed upon him by all in Shreveport and Pine Bluff. Mr. Greenblatt was very kind to us and we return our thanks to the reverend gentleman.

The present minister of Shreveport, Rev. Mr. Hess, to whom we had only a formal introduction (he having been very busy in some of his official duties), we learn has been lately selected and seems to give satisfaction. We regret that we had not the opportunity of being better acquainted with the reverend, and thereby deprived of saying anything about him.

Owing to our short stay in Shreveport, we are unable to give a description of this beautiful city with all her advantages and accommodations, and suffice it to say, that Shreveport, the second largest city in Louisiana, is doing a vast amount of business and seems to be a thriving and lively place.

Our Israelites here, have done their full duty in matters appertaining to Judaism—and we find here a congregation, "Hebrew Zion," with Mr. Levy as President, doing well and flourishing—we learn that this congregation next to New Orleans, has the handsomest temple within the South, and we regret that we could not see it, so as to give an elaborate description of the same. Mr. Levy who has been president of the congregation for the past nine years, is exerting himself and doing all within his power, in his usual courteous and kind manner, to uphold the same, to the pride of all Israelites.

We also find here a Louisiana I. O. B. B. Lodge, with Bro. M. J. Goldsmith President; a K. S. B. [Kesher Shel Barzel] Lodge, with Louis Levy, President; and I. F. S. of I. [Independent Order of Free Sons of Israel], with Bro. Broedning as President, all working harmoniously and are in good circumstances. There is also here a Ladies Benevolent Association, with Mrs. H. Winter, President, bestowing charities and aiding the needy, whenever called upon— we are unable to give the names of the officers of these ladies societies and asking their pardon trust that our contributor will name them in his next communication.

Wednesday noon the shrilling and loud whistle of the Steamer *Danube* reminded us, that the time for our departure has arrived and bidding adieu to all our friends, we embarked and soon found ourselves with the soft breezes, flapping of sails, and air of steam, gliding down the Red River, and in company of the cultured and agreeable gentleman, Mr. Obedlike, passed our time pleasantly, reached Alexandria Thursday evening, and became the guest of Bro. Ed. Weil.

Alexandria, a city of about four thousand inhabitants, situated on the banks of the Red River, is quite a business place and our Israelites numbering about one hundred and fifty souls, and about twenty families are carrying on an extensive business, and are very much respected by the Gentiles. Many of them hold responsible positions. Our host, Mr. Ed. Weil has been honored with the mayorality of the city; Jonas Rosenthal, a member of their city council and Mr. Moses Rosenthal is Treasurer of the Rapides Parish—all holding their functions to the satisfaction of all.

Alexandria Congregation, with Bro. E. Weil as President and Rev. Marx Klein as reader, is in healthy condition; in their magnificent and gorgeous temple, services are regularly held Friday evening and Saturday morning. We were delighted with the beautiful music and singing produced by the sweet tenor voice of Mr. Klein assisted by the excellent choir, composed by Mrs. L. Ehrstein, Misses Julia Gutman, L. Weil, Fannie Levine, Bessy Lehman, and C. Weil and Messrs. Moses Blum and Isaac Sackman. These ladies and gentlemen are aiding vastly to the attraction and beauty of the services; their singing is admired by all who hear them. We lectured Friday and Saturday night in the temple to an appreciative audience of Jew and Gentile, and hope that our words of Friday lecture will be remembered by the members of the congregation at the next annual election.

Sunday morning we visited the Sunday School, found there about thirty-five children, well disciplined and advanced in their studies. Upon request, we addressed the children, whom we found very attentive to our remarks. Mr. Julius Levine, is Superintendent of the Sunday School, and the gentleman with his untiring zeal and energy in behalf of the progress and advancement of the children, as well as for elevation of Judaism, is doing a vast deal of good, and merits the appreciation of all. He is assisted by Rev. Mr. Klein, Misses Julia Goodman, Bessie Lehman, Carroline Weil, and Mr. A. Zaer, all of whom are attending punctually to their duty and aid materially in the labor of love.

There is also here a Rebecca Lodge I. O. B. B., with Bro. E. Weil as President (whose place is now filled by Bro. Klein), and is progressing finely. We visited it and addressed the brethren.

Our ladies here, "God bless them," they also are contributing their might and have formed a Ladies Hebrew Society, with the following officers: Mrs. D. Lehman, President; Mrs. I. Levine, Vice President; Mrs. Chas. Goldberg, Secretary; and Mrs. Dr. Rosenthal, Treasurer. They have assisted greatly toward the accomplishment of the building of the temple, and are doing generally a vast deal of good.

We remained here until Monday, our stay having been made very pleasant and agreeable by our brothers.

Our host and his most esteemed family have placed us under many obligations, and we shall ever remember the pleasant hours spent among them.

Monday noon the steamer *Silver City* arrived and taking leave of all our friends, we departed for the Crescent City, where we arrived Wednesday and found our associates and friends pleased to meet us, and with a hearty welcome we were once more seated in the office of the *Jewish South*, 46 Camp Street.

C. W.

Letter Number Twenty

Charles Wessolowsky to Rabbi Edward B. M. Browne

St. Louis, Missouri
September 1879

• • •

[*Wessolowsky discusses in detail how the Jewish High Holidays are observed in the St. Louis' Hebrew congregations of Shaare Emeth, United Congregation, B'nai El and Sheeres Israel.*]

• • •

ויאמר הנני [82]

Here we are in the "Mound City," the metropolis of the West, viewing her gigantic structures, her elegant and magnificent edifices, beautiful and palatial residences, handsome and unique parks, superb places of amusement including the lager beer gardens and saloons which are very numerous, the throng of people constantly running to and fro, the busy life exhibited in all streets and corners, the tastefully and elegantly attired ladies promenading Fourth Street with their smiling and joyful faces, expressing their approbation of a satisfaction with the new designs and styles of dress goods and other kinds of wares, so richly displayed in the large and most artistically arranged show windows, all attentively examining on opening days which or what would be to the greatest advantage to their complexion and figure, and we indeed realized the words of Mr. Greely, "young man go west," but when we leave this great thoroughfare, "the Broadway of St. Louis," plant ourselves in a by-street, we and others are accosted by poor beggarly looking children, asking us for alms to satisfy perhaps their hunger, which they must suffer in their parental house; and when those miserable, innocent children in their pitiful

---

[82]Pronounced veh-ah-moe hee-nay-nee, which means "And he said, 'Here I am'." This "Hineni" prayer is symbolic of the position that the Jew is ready for anything that is demanded of him by God. It embodies the petition that man, unworthy as the sinner he is, may pray in a manner acceptable to God. The "Hineni" prayer is read during the penitential holidays of the New Year and the Day of Atonement as a statement of readiness to repent for sins, and accept judgement of actions taken during the previous year.

tones meet the cold marble heart of someone, he or she with a glance of scorn and contempt frighten that poor being away from their presence, when this two-fold picture of life is presented to us; we pause and ask ourselves: Is not, after all, the South a blessed country, where no such heart-rending scenes are seen in the street, and where the poor, in their state of misery and sorrow are not exposed to cold charity of the passerby, and not subject to those insolvent contemptuous looks and replies, which, alas, they meet so often in the large cities North and West?

Our brothers who are here in large numbers, are also aiding vastly to the grandeur and elegance of this, the rival city of Chicago, and many of them are carrying on extensive manufacturing, wholesale and retail business, and are also large property holders. Many of our rising generations have deviated from the path of their parents, embark in various professions, and thereby, with their progress, skill and talent, demonstrate clearly to the eye of all, that the Jew is well-fitted for any position and vocation in life; and that in the field of literature, law, medicine or any other profession he acquires name and fame, as well as he accumulates wealth in the regular vocation as a business man.

In our next letter we will inform our readers, most extensively, upon this point, and endeavor to give them the name of all prominent Israelites within this city.

How the Holidays Were Kept.

Weeks before the approach of the past eventful days to Judaism, we could see Rabbi, Reader and Sexton, all busily engaged with their necessary preparations, the one with his sermons, the other with his music, and the other with supplying the demand for seats in his respective Temple, as all Israel is expected to meet his God on those days and is to mingle in religious communion with his co-religionists. Although thousands of the sons and daughters of Israel who never enter God's temple at any other time, and never find time to hear the preacher expounding their truthful religion, and his words of admonition and reproof, yet on this annual revival, the synagogues and temples are filled by those very men, who, either from fear or other cause, think they must seek on those days the presence of God, although neglected on all other days, and that the Israelite can discharge his duty when he parades his piety on that holiday and indulges in sentimental observance of the same. Alas, such is the deplorable state of Judaism nowadays, and maybe, who is wiser than we are to solve the problem, "why is it so"?

Temple Shaare Emeth.[83]

On the morning of the New Year,[84] we found ourselves winding our way towards Pine and 17th Streets, where a handsome, spacious and gorgeous temple beautifies that corner, and as we entered we were indeed startled by the multitude of visitors assembled therein. Every seat occupied and hundreds of Israelites were standing participating in the service, listening attentively to the sweet and melodious tunes of the choir, composed of about fourteen voices with a musical director to lead them, and we exclaimed with David, "I rejoiced when they said unto me, let us go in the house of the Lord." Rev. Dr. Sonneshine who is the spiritual guide of this strictly reformed congregation delivered a lecture in the German language upon "life being a dream."[85] This gentleman, well-known all throughout the United States as an eloquent and pathetic orator, has a special faculty in wielding the eloquence of his great mind with grace and power, which forces his hearers to arouse their feelings and to bring them into close communion with that divinity which is in himself. Learned and unlearned alike, are bestowing their praises upon this great man's oratorical powers, and it is needless to say, recognize in him one of the great orators of this country.

We also visited this temple on Yom Kippur[86] eve and morning, heard

---

[83]*Shaare Emeth* (pronounced sha-rah em-cth) means "Gates of Truth."

[84]The Jewish New Year is called *Rosh Hashanah* (pronounced Rowsh-ha-sha-nah) which means "head of the year." This holiday begins a cycle of special holidays. It introduces the Ten Days of Repentance, when Jews examine their souls and take stock of their past actions. The tradition is that on the New Year God sits in judgment on humanity and listens to prayer and repentance. This holiday and that of the Day of Atonement may be considered the climax of Jewish worship. In them the most important ideals are expressed: the sovereignty of God and the brotherhood of man; reward and punishment for blessings and sins; and restoration in Zion where a center of peace and enlightenment for all mankind shall be created. On these days, it is the desire of the Jew to rise above the daily routine. For this reason, these days are dedicated entirely to worship and meditation.

[85]From Wessolowsky's comments one might assume that the ability to speak English or the ability of the congregants to understand English even as late as 1879 is rare enough to be noted in admirable terms. The need to utilize the German vernacular may be an indication of the short time many of the congregants had been in this country in numbers large enough to necessitate the use of German in both liturgy and sermon.

[86]*Yom Kippur* (pronounced yom-key-poor) is the Day of Atonement. It ends the Ten Days of Repentance, at which time—tradition says—the Book of Life is

both lectures, and while we again express our admiration for the gentleman's greatness and eloquence yet we thought that in hearing the theme of his lecture of the eve of Yom Kippur, he did not do justice to himself.

Temple United Congregation

This is a handsome, magnificent synagogue, situation on Sixth Street and carried on in a conservative mode of worship.[87] We attended therein the service of New Year's Eve and Yom Kippur. The attendance was unusually large. Rev. Dr. Messing, the Rabbi of said congregation performing the service as reader also, and was ably assisted by an excellent and efficient choir, composed of a quartette, who added largely to the beauty and solemnity of the service. The reverend gentleman, although young in years, possesses great qualifications in lecturing in the German language, and while we admire his lecture on New Year's Eve, which indeed was very suitable and to the point, the one at *Neelah*,[88] we thought was grand, and handled in masterly manner. Messing, as a candid, pure and frank rabbi, eager to uphold the tenets and doctrines of Judaism in a conservative mode, deserves great credit, and indeed labors very hard for the progress and elevation of Israel. The congregation contemplates selling this temple and building one in a more suitable location, as there are many Israelites residing in the upper portion of the city who would gladly join, if the temple would be situated nearer to their residence. Upon request we aided the doctor in officiating partly on Yom Kippur, and we hereby take occasion to thank the officers of the Temple Shaare Emeth and United Hebrew Congregation for courtesies extended to us during those days.

Temple B'nai El.[89]

We regret to say that we as yet had no opportunity to visit this elegant

---

sealed by God. It is regarded as the holiest day in the year and is marked by a 24-hour fasting period, and in orthodox circles by 24 hours of liturgy without any break.

[87]Wessolowsky used this term to refer to the moderates in the Reform Movement who stood between the orthodox on one hand and the extreme Reformers on the other hand.

[88]*Neelah* (pronounced knee-lah), the Concluding Service, is the final ritual of the Yom Kippur service. It means "closing" because it refers to the closing of the gates of heaven at the end of the Day of Atonement upon the rendering of final judgement of God as inscribed in the Book of Life.

[89]*B'nai El* (pronounced beh-nay-el) means "Son of God."

structure, located on Choteau Avenue. We have met Rev. Mr. Spitz, the officiating minister, and found him to be a clever and courteous gentleman and trust that we will have occasion to give a full and detailed statement of this congregation and its officers at a future day. We learn from those that were present at the services of the holidays that they were much pleased and appreciate the labors and services of the reverend gentleman.

Hall of Congregation Sheeres Israel.[90]

This hall is used as a place of worship by a congregation called the "Krakauer Congregation,"[91] Rev. S. H. Jacobs, Minister of Beth El Emeth[92] congregation of Memphis, and who is now here as a refugee, officiated during the holidays. The services were conducted in strictly orthodox style, and there was a numerous attendance. We heard the Reverend gentleman read *Musaph*[93] on the second day of New Year, and we were reminded of the days of our youth, when we attended similar service, conducted by our great Cantor in our native place. The gentleman gave various lectures which were appreciated by those who heard them.

There were other small *Cheveres*[94] where amateurs here officiated, but we are unable to give an account of the same, suffice it to say that all were filled with visitors, all ready to atone for their past sins, and willing to start out anew to debit their accounts until the next great day, when they believe credit will be given them, and thereby accounts balanced.

We have met a large number of Southern friends from all parts of Mississippi, Arkansas, and Tennessee, particularly from Memphis, as a great many have refuged to this place. We are told that over 6,000 people

---

[90]*Sheeres Israel* (pronounced share-es is-ree-al) means "Remnants of Israel."

[91]The term *Krakauer* refers to the point of origin of the members of the congregation who immigrated from Krakau in Galicia which at that time was a southern portion of Poland that have been incorporated into the Austrian Empire.

[92]*Beth El Emeth* (pronounced beth-el-eh-meth) means "Place of God's Truth."

[93]*Musaph* or *musaf* (pronounced moo-sah-f) is part of the congregational prayers. It is an "additional service" performed after morning service on Sabbaths, the festivals and the New Moon days in commemoration of the additional sacrifice offered at the Temple on those days (Num. 28:9). It is performed following the reading of the Torah.

[94]*Cheveres* refers to small groups of orthodox Jews who joined together for learning and prayer. Traditionally such groups were not formal congregations, but were large enough to satisfy quorum requirements. They were usually study groups who intermixed prayer and learning.

from Memphis are here. We wish that they may be able to soon return to their peaceful homes and that the dread plague [the yellow fever epidemic] now visiting their city and any other unpleasantness may never cause them to depart.

We were pleased to meet the editorial staff and proprietors of the *Jewish Tribune*, to whom we offer our acknowledgement for attentions paid us.

Also, our old comrades, playmates of our youth, whom we were glad once more to see and to know that they are numbered among the living.

C. W.

Letter Number Twenty-One

Charles Wessolowsky to Rabbi Edward B. M. Browne

St. Louis, Missouri
7 October 1879

• • •

[*Wessolowsky describes in detail a benefit for the yellow fever sufferers of Memphis given by the Hebrew Young Men's Literary Association; he next offers a biographical sketch of Evelyn Spyer.*]

• • •

To be charitable and generous is the peculiar and distinct quality of a Jew, characteristic of our race; and this character was exhibited in its highest measure by our Israelites of this city, who, prompted by their natural innate feelings of benevolence, attended *en masse* a grand entertainment given by the Hebrew Young Men's Association, for the benefit of the yellow fever sufferers of Memphis, at Harmonie Hall on Saturday, October 4th. And although with the thermometer soaring in the nineties, an evening at a place which contains large audiences is not an enjoyable experience, yet the hall was filled to its utmost capacity by a large and fashionable audience, who were eager and anxious to aid in this noble cause—to bestow their assistance upon those poor and stricken sufferers in that unfortunate city. The program for the evening's entertainment was very attractive, and all credit is due to the managers for the elegant selections.

The following is a copy of the same:

1. Overture - "Pique Dome" - Suppe ... Messrs. Epstein Bors., Stueck and Bohn
2. Address .... Nath. Myers
3. So rano solo - "Judith" - Collcone ....
   Miss T. Rosenheim
4. Recitation - "Fall of the Pemberton Mills" ....
   Miss Evelyn Spyer
   An intensely interesting description of the falling of a colossal Mill, whereby nearly 700 operatives lost their lives.

5. Violin solo........... Mr. I. Schoen accompanied by
   Mr. A. J. Epstein
6. Schiller's "Lay of the Bell"........Richard Walheim
Illustrated by Tableaux Vivants:

a) Labor - Arbeit
b) Departure - Abachied
c) Return - Rueckehr

g) Fire - Feuer
h) After the Fire - Nach dem
   Feuer
i) Harvest Festival -
   Erntefest

d) Love - Liebe
e) Wedding - Huchaeit
f) Mother's Care - Muiter
   Waltch
j) Peace - Friede
k) Revolution - Revolution

l) Crowning of the Bell -
   Concordis

Messrs. Epstein Bros., known as artists of great fame, performed the overture in their usual skillful and talented manner which, from the applause given, was received by the audience with great favor.

The address of Mr. Nathan Myers, an Attorney at Law, of renown, was delivered in a clear and distinct voice, in a happy and humorous mode pleasing to everyone. His subject: "The growth of the spirit of philanthropy," was perfectly exhausted, demonstrating distinctly, that while centuries ago mankind was blunt to all humane feelings, and exposed to all cruelties, insults and whimsical laws of a ruler of a country, and subject to the different punishments inflicted on the various countries (even those that today are called the most civilized) and the slay glittering [probably intended "slay guttering-unimpeded destruction] of human lives, for the gratification of him who was in power, today not alone life and liberty are guarded by nearly the whole civilized world, but even societies are formed for the protection of animals, and so watchful and humane are these gentlemen in the performances of their duties, that even the beating of an egg is considered an inhumane act. Mr. Myers then proceeded to show the spirit of philanthropy now existing, the many acts of kindness and love now performed; and closed with an appeal to the members of the Association to uphold their institution, to aid in the intellectual and moral development of its members and strive in the fulfillment of its end, the good of mankind.

The address was very much admired, and the audience expressed loudly their appreciation.

The solo, "Judith," sung by Miss Tillie Rosenheim, was indeed charming and heavenly. The young lady having full control of her sweet and melodious voice, and her singing was a very attractive feature of the evening's amusement. Also the violin solo, by Mr. Schoen, who seems to be master of his instrument, was rendered skillfully and artistically—both were very much appreciated by the audience and Miss Rosenheim was the recipient of many bouquets of flowers.

But the most pleasing feature of the evening to our taste was the recitation of "Fall of the Pemberton Mills," by Evelyn Spyer, a wonder child of ten years of age. Dressed in a beautiful costume of white, her luxuriant hair hanging gracefully over her shoulders and down the back; her eyes keen and glittering and with the sweet and amiable expression of her mouth, she indeed looked charming and lovely, and we thought that everything necessary and essential for the combination of charms in one person is centered in her, and that this "Wonder of Wonders" looked more angelic than human. As she appeared upon the stage, tremendous applause greeted her, and after acknowledging the enthusiasm of the audience, she proceeded to recite the above poem. Her wonderful delivery, vivid, distinct, and forcible, her thorough understanding of the force of language, her elocutionary powers, strong mellow and developed voice, her clear articulation, her gestures almost beyond criticism, are indeed marvelous, astonishing and are almost beyond belief even in this age of wonders.

The audience was completely carried away by this "wonder child," and at the conclusion of her first recitation, she was enthusiastically encored and in response gave the "dying scene of Juliet," from Romeo and Juliet in the same finished and artistic style that characterized her first effort, and she was loaded with floral tokens.

For the information of our readers we have gathered the following biographical items of the greatest elocutionary phenomenon.

Evelyn Spyer, the only daughter of Dr. and Mrs. Joe Spyer of this city, reached the age of ten on the twenty-seventh day of August, 1879. When she was but two months old her parents removed to Brazil and at six years of age she returned to her native city, St. Louis, and in a few weeks spoke the English language as fluently as other children, who were living here all their lives. She is very fond of reading and passionately so of Shakespeare. She possesses a phenomenal memory, so that two readings of a poem of moderate length is all she requires to retain it in her memory and she certainly understands her authors.

In Kirkwood, Mo., when but six years of age she first appeared before the public—the occasion was a literary entertainment, and she recited "The Dying Alchemist"—with wonderful effect, and startled her hearers then into expressions of great surprise. Since then she received many invitations to partake in entertainments of dramatic character, and on each occasion, she won fresh praises from the press and the people; and today she is as famous as an actress of unsurpassed merit and ability, possessing by nature extraordinary dramatic insight and great power of expression.

Well may St. Louis be proud of this rising star, and no less we Israelites, for she is a Jewish child, of Jewish parentage and raised as such.

We learn that in recognition of her marvelous abilities the city of St. Louis through the Mayor offered her a benefit and she realized the handsome sum of thirteen hundred dollars. We were shown letters wherein companies offer to engage her at five hundred dollars per week. May she ever continue to be the pride and wonder of the age.

Schiller's "Lay on the Bell," (Die Glocke) recited in German by Richard Walheim and illustrated by Tableaux vivants was quite interesting, the representation original, well gotten up and reflecting great credit upon the managers, although the chimes of this bell, did not produce that constant and harmonic sound which we have heard given at the recitation of "Die Glocke" before.

At eleven o'clock the audience dispersed highly pleased with their evening amusement and bestowing laudatory praises upon the performers and managers and wishing for a speedy return of such an enjoyable evening.

From thence in company of some ladies and gentlemen we started to "Tony Faust's" and, reader, to know him is to be acquainted with the most liberal, enterprising, gallant and unselfish man in the city of St. Louis. The gentleman does not deal in Me-susas[95] but carries on the finest and most fashionable restaurant and

---

[95]Normally spelled *mezuzah* (pronounced meh-zoo-zah), it is a small

lager beer saloon in this or any other city. He is well patronized by all, as the most fastidious are able to satisfy their epicurism at this magnificent establishment, which is so arranged and situated that in the midst of summer and heat of lager a person is able to keep cool. Had we the space and the descriptive powers of Dickens we would gladly undertake to acquaint our readers with the location and architecture of the building, and to give them a faint idea of these elegant statues and beautiful and fragrant flowers, artistically arranged in the upper portion of the building; alas, we lack of both, and therefore, must satisfy outselves to tell our readers that to know and to see the finest establishment of this kind is, if you ever come to St. Louis, to visit "Tony Faust," with my assurance that your pockets will never be as heavy when you leave the place as when you came in—What, Never?—hardly ever.

As we promenaded Fourth Street, we were very agreeably surprised in meeting Rev. Dr. Suhler, formally minister of Dallas, Texas, who is here with his very interesting family en route for Vicksburg, Miss., where he has been elected successor of the late Dr. Gothelf. We were glad to hear that the reverend gentleman is pleased with his new position (and who will not be pleased in Vicksburg), and we congratulate the Yehudim [Hebrews] there of having had the opportunity to elect such a pure and savant Rabbi as Mr. Suhler is, who is well worthy to lay upon his shoulders the priestly robe of his predecessor. We hope that he and his family may arrive safely at their place of destination, and we feel satisfied that Mr. Suhler knows how to appreciate the "Vicksburg Congregation." More anon.

C. W.

P. S. We ask pardon of our readers for not fulfilling our promise "to

---

parchment scroll affixed to the doorpost of rooms as enjoined in Deut. 6:9 and again in 11:20: "and you shall write them (words of God) on the doorposts of your house and on the gates of your cities." It consists of a parchment made from the skins of a clean animal upon which passages are written from Deut. 6:4-9 and Deut. 11:13-21, traditionally in 22 lines. The parchment is rolled up and inserted in a case with a small aperture on the back. On the back of the parchment is written the word *shadai* (or *shaddai*) which means "(the) Almighty." It is then affixed to the right-hand, inward-slanting doorpost of a house. Also see note 77 above.

give them a statement of all institutions here, and names of prominent Jews," in this letter, as we thought the above will be of like interest, but we shall endeavor to make it good in the future.

C. W.

Letter Number Twenty-two

Charles Wessolowsky to Rabbi Edward B. M. Browne

St. Louis, Missouri
15 October 1879

• • •

[*Wessolowsky discusses the Hebrew Relief Society of St. Louis; he describes how the Jewish holiday of Simchas Torah is celebrated; he also describes a fund-raising fair held by Temple B'nai El.*]

• • •

The "Veiled Prophet" has passed, and with it all anxieties, hopes, expectations, and promises, of fun and pleasure are averted. The St. Louis fair is now counted among those things that were, and we once more can promenade on the Fourth and other streets without being in danger of being squeezed like a lemon, and shoved from one place to another like a baseball. The multitude of people attending the fair have all returned to their peaceful homes, satisfied with what they have seen, and reckoning up the dollars that were spent, and the "Mound City," people are now thinking, and studying and meditating what best to procure and to arrange next so that the stranger in St. Louis can find attraction, fun and merryment, and be enticed to visit the city in large numbers. A fair of course is for the advancement of art, mechanisms of all kinds, agriculture, etc., and the western people are wide awake for the promotion of all that is aiding civilization and is of interest to mankind.

Hebrew Relief Society.

By that name we find a society here in the city, to which all congregations, associations and other kindred institutions contribute their might, and the funds of said society are managed by a board of directors who alternately meet at their office daily, to attend to the wants of those indigent persons who are so unfortunate as to be compelled to ask for alms of their fellow men. This society certainly deserves the praise and commendation of everyone, and is worthy of imitation by all large cities. Last Sunday an election was held for several directors, whose time of office has expired, and although we have not learned who the gentlemen are that carried off the victory, yet we are satisfied that the officers were properly divided among all institutions respectively, as each is certainly entitled to its proportionate share of honor, otherwise the old cry "taxation without representation" may arise and be perhaps detrimental to the good feeling and progress of the said society.

Simchas Torah.[96]

Although the holidays have passed and everyone who fasted[97] now feels stimulated and invigorated from the feast and festivities of our Succoth,[98] yet we cannot refrain from mentioning a scene which to our pleasure we beheld on Simchas Torah eve in the synagogue of the United Congregation on 6th Street, Dr. Messing officiating. After the regular services were read, about one hundred and fifty children, each with a small United States flag in their hands headed by the Rabbi, officers and others, each bearing the scroll, marched three times around down the left and returning on the right aisle, chanting suitable and beautiful hymns and responded to by the efficient and excellent choir.

It was, indeed, a grand sight, awakening the memories of the good old days, where everyone of us rejoiced on the eve of the feast

---

[96]*Simchas* (or *Simhath*) *Torah* (pronounced sim-chaas, with a gutteral -ch, toe-rah) literally means "the rejoicing of the law." A joyous holiday, it celebrates the reading of the last portion of the year's cycle of reading of the Torah, and the beginning of a new cycle with the reading of the first portion of Genesis.

[97]This refers to the fast during *Yom Kippur*, as an emphasis of the day's solemnity and total dedication to worship, a 24-hour fasting period. The fasting is not done out of any sense of penalty or physical infliction. It is done as a reminder of the importance of prayer and as a fortification against the temptation of everyday life encroaching on contemplation. It is taken as a conquest of the demands of our physical life by the need for communion with God. It is not an act to promote misery or despair. To the contrary, by Jewish law, if fasting in any way threatens one's health, that person is prohibited from fasting.

[98]*Succos* (or *Sukkoth* or *Succoth*) (pronounced sue-kos) is the festival of Tabernacles (or Booths). It is a seven-day holiday, emphasizing the theme of thanksgiving. It is highlighted by the construction of a *succah* (or *sukkah*), a temporary structure with a roof, usually made of branches, through which one must see the sky. From this roof hangs all sorts of fruit. It is the holiday on which one rejoices in the granting of the law.

of Torah;[99] and we were glad to see those children imbued with the idea and knowledge of the ceremony of this holiday, and to feel happy and joyful at the occasion. After all were seated, the Doctor, who had honored us with delivering the Simchas Torah oration, introduced us with very appropriate remarks to the audience, and we addressed first the children, then the older folks, upon the feast of Torah of ancient days and that of modern times.

Then each of the children were presented by Mr. Cohen, the President, with a beautiful package of candy and all left for home merry and happy, feeling that they as Jewish children have also a feast where they receive presents and made to feel glad and not be envious and jealous of the Christmas of our Gentile children.

In the morning the regular ceremony was kept up and Mr. Plou, as the recipient of the honor of חתן בראשית[100] and Mr. Werner of חתן תורה[101] were rejoiced and demonstrated the same by having their friends to share of liberality and hospitality, particularly the latter, who gave a feast fitting for the gods of old, where wine and everything else that gladdens the heart made one feel and wish for the return of the old social days where such occurrences were often and where everyone participating, offered freely and not hypocritically his share to the joy and happiness of the occasion. Both of these gentlemen will please accept our thanks for being numbered among our friends.

---

[99]During the service, after the Torah is taken out of the ark, a procession ensues in which a circuit is made by all members of the congregation, who carry a bough from four plants and chant the *Hoshanos* (or *Hoshana*) (pronounced ha-shah-nas), the Prayers for Salvation. In the course of time, the procession expanded from merely circuiting the altar to that of walking around the entire sanctuary with all members following the person carrying the Torah. Traditionally, seven circuits are made and the honor of carrying the Torah during any one of them is a great one. In many congregations, particularly small ones, everyone is allowed an opportunity of carrying the Torah.

[100]Pronounced ha-san toe-ra. It is the honored duty of reading the last portion of the Torah during the festival of *Simchas* (or *Simhath*) *Torah*. Also see note 96 above.

[101]Pronounced ha-san beh-ray-shees. It is the sought-after honor of reading the beginning passages in Genesis and starting again the cycle of the year's readings of the Torah. The recipient of this and the previous honor are required by tradition to give parties marking the joyous event.

B'nai El Fair.

For many years a debt of considerable amount was hanging over this congregation, and for the purpose of defraying the same, a fair was arranged and the exhibition continued for three successive nights. Harmony Club Hall was transformed into a Bazaar, decorated in an elegant and handsome manner, and the daughters of Israel with their many attractions and fascinations, buttonholing the gentlemen present, bewitched them into taking chances on everything, from a pin cushion to a handsome silver set.

There were fifteen tables covered with fancy goods and presided over by many of our charming Jewesses; a post office, with a captivating postmistress and a Rebecca's well; all of them doing excellent business, and the whole seems to be a perfect success. We regret than we cannot give names of all our pretty Jewesses, who worked so energetically in behalf of this laudable enterprise, neither are we able to give an elaborate description of the decorations, adornments and magnificence of the hall; suffice to say, that the whole had a pompous and splendid appearance, exhibiting grandeur, and was admired by all visitors. Not wishing to singularize, nor to be partial to one lady (as we admire all ladies), yet we must say that we never beheld a fairer and more fascinating Rebecca at any well, drawing water, lemonade or any other liquid than this Rebecca and we hope that she has charmed some Isaac by giving him and his camels to drink. We were pleased to meet at the fair, assisting Rebecca, Miss Siechel, a cousin of "Joshua," from Macon, Ga., with whom we spent an agreeable hour.

We trust that a sufficient amount will be realized to liquidate the debt; as certainly the undertaking deserves all credit and success.

Jacobs Patent Lithogram

Walking down Fourth Street, our curiosity was aroused by a lady who was exhibiting something to a multitude of people, who seemed to be amazed and surprised; and upon inquiry we soon ascertained that the cause of the excitement was "Jacobs Patent Lithogram." A new invention for producing facsimiles of circulars, notes, etc., without the aid of any prepared paper or anything else and any boy can operate it with a few minutes instruction. We examined the same and found it to be very useful and simple in its operation. Fifty copies can be procured of any writing, from one original; and all that is required is an impression tablet, a bottle of Jacob's ink, and a sponge.

From the name we presume the inventor is a Jew, and we asked ourselves whether Mr. Corbin will admit him to the Manhattan Beach? Perhaps he is the "only white Jew."

Mr. Spiro formerly of Helena, Ark., intends to locate himself here in St. Louis. We were glad to meet the gentleman and wish him success.

We were also very much pleased to shake hands with Gabriel Meier, Esq., from Peoria, Ill., the celebrated Jewish lawyer, who is on a visit to this city. Mr. Meier is a savant and courteous gentleman, who will make friends everywhere. More anon.

C. W.

Letter Number Twenty-Three

Charles Wessolowsky to Rabbi Edward B. M. Browne

St. Louis, Missouri
23 October 1879

• • •

[*Wessolowsky discusses Jewish liturgical music; next he discusses the role the press should take in improving Jewish-Gentile relations; and finally, he mentions Max Mierson's book on commercial law.*]

• • •

In a city like St. Louis with a population of a half million and upward, with daily occurrences, and mighty happenings, a city of numerous and various institutions, full of gossip, rumor and circulating reports, a newspaper may find many items of interest, recording all the suicides, homicides, and other sights of startling news, yet for a Jewish paper it is rather a difficult task, to find Jewish-interesting items, which would engage the attention and curiosity of our general readers, and therefore we must ask the indulgence of all who peruse this correspondence to be forbearing and patient with us; and to the critic we say : "let he who is free from sins, cast the first stone."

It was our good fortune to form the acquaintance of Mr. G. S. Ensel, of Springfield, Ill., a gentleman of culture and refinement, who kindly has shown us his gigantic work styled "Ancient Liturgical Music; or the Liturgy of the Jewish, Christian and Mohammedan Worship." In it the gentleman gives an elaborate and full description of the various kinds of ancient musical instruments, at the same time correcting the erroneous translations of the Septuagint, Luther, and King James of those portions of the Bible, where musical instruments are mentioned, and giving the proper musical sense of the same. Mr. Ensel also treats upon the music of the Hebrews during the time of the Temple, quoting Talmudical authorities and also upon the musical liturgy of the post-biblical period, giving the history of the compilation of the Machsur,[102] and

---

[102]Sometimes spelled *mazor* (or *mahzor*) (pronounced mah-zore) meaning "cycle." It is the festival prayerbook as distinguished from the daily prayerbook.

answering the question, where and how our old Chasonim [cantors] got their ancient melodies and tunes, and the ever-increasing Pejutim פּיוטים [103] Selichaus סליחות[104] and Kinaus קינות[105] Mr. Ensel proves historically and by copious musical manuscripts, that the so-called traditional music of the synagogue is obtained from two sources: First, "oriental origin," comparing it with the music of Arabia, Phoenicia, Armania [Armenia], and African colonists, and with the hymns of the earliest Christian church, represented mainly by St. Ambrose and his Syriac predecessors.[106] The second, that of the secular music of the early and middle ages had been introduced in Europe by the crusaders and showing clearly by many examples given, that the Sephatic[107] and Armoric melodies to their ritual were derived from the "Troubadour of the Province;" while the Jewish liturgy of the north obtained its tunes from the secular music of the nations among whom they lived, and the so-called Polish Chazan [cantor] is a faithful representative of the slavonic folk-sounds, and so is the German ritual the efflux of German secular music. Mr. Ensel also compares the Jewish music with that of the Christian

---

[103]Sometimes spelled *piyyutim* (pronounced pea-u-team) meaning "poetry." These are lyrical compositions designed to embellish obligatory prayers or other religious ceremonies during the congregational services in the synagogue and temple.

[104]Pronounced seh-lich-ows with a guttural -ch. It literally means "forgiveness." Like the *piyyut* and *Kinaus, Selichaus* is one of the divisions of poetical selections for the ritual service. These verses are prayers and poems requesting God to pardon our sins and end our "suffering." Most of these prayers were written between the 7th and 17th centuries and have been incorporated into the synagogue services, especially those of the New Year and the Day of Atonement.

[105]Pronounced as written, kin-ows. The poems in the division of the *Kinaus* are different from those in *Selichaus* in content. These poems and verses are restricted to expressions of deep sorrow and mourning over the loss of independence, the loss of the homeland, the fall of the Temple, and the dispersion of Israel.

[106]St. Ambrose (339-397) was the Bishop of Milan (beginning in 374) as well as civil governor of the province, who excommunicated the Emperor Theodosius for allowing his troops to massacre a mob in Thessalonica, and compelled him to do penance, thereby laying down the cornerstone of the principle "priests judge emperors."

[107]Sometimes spelled Sephardic. It literally means "Spaniard." The customs, rituals, synagogue services, and Hebrew pronunciation differ from those of the Jews of Germany and Eastern Europe.

church and looking over the same, we were reminded of the old "Wie es juedeld se Christend es sich" [It is as old as Christianity itself] for we found many Jewish melodies to be similar to those of the Christian church and vice versa. Another interesting feature of this valuable work is the appendix giving the historical developments of musical notation from the earliest times to our present system.

This work is not yet finished, although Mr. Ensel has labored for the past ten years, in the research of all that may give him the least information, and he thinks that it will yet occupy him at least five years before he will be able to complete the same in the manner that he wishes, and in the meantime, Mr. Ensel proposes to bring his work to the notice of the public by lecturing upon the same subjects, and will therefore accept invitations to lecture, from any charitable institutions or society that may wish to avail itself of the opportunity. We will add that the gentleman serves voluntarily in the capacity of Minister and Reader in the reformed congregation at Springfield, Ill., and that his ministerial labors as well as the accomplishments of these enormous great works, heretofore mentioned, are for the elevation of Judaism, and that it is his intention and desire, that the ancient Jewish melodies, may be preserved, by modernizing the same; and introduced in our synagogue, with a suitable ritual, and hymns. We wish the gentleman all the success he deserves and that the world will give him the due appreciation which he so richly merits.

We were rather surprised the other morning, reading the "specials to the *Republicans*" headed "Choice Scandals in Jewish Circles in New York," as we thought enlightened Christians, especially journalists, have long since buried their crooked prejudice, towards the Jew and that the name of party or parties is sufficient to be paraded before the public without giving his or her religion and that an Israelite overstepping perchance the lines of morality, and which is of very rare occurrence compared with others, could be brought before the public without stating his religion, as well as Mr. Jones or Mr. Smith's daily crimes are heralded throughout the land without saying whether he is a Baptist or an Episcopalian.

In this enlightened century, and especially in this city, where Jew and Gentile meet, willing to be united into one common brotherhood (as have we not all one Father?) bigotry and narrow-mindedness should be superseded by liberality and impartiality, and journalists in the performance of their duties, should well bear in mind that the Jew, who is their liberal patron, is possessed of refined feelings and pride as much as others, and that it does not meet with his taste, to see his religion or race brought in connection with a scandal. The press, which ought to be the church, pulpit, and preacher, should, by their examples, teach others to eradicate the long-harbored feelings of prejudice and hatred; and to tell the public that the dark ages are now illumed by the exalted idea, that Jew and Gentile are children of one God, and that both amenable to the same laws, have but one common duty to perform, and that no distinction, no greater honor can be conferred upon one or the other for reason of his religion; and what is seemingly not proper and not used by the one, ought not to be done by and to the other.

Mr. A. Franklin, of Memphis, Tenn., who is a refuge to this city, was presented with a handsome gold-headed cane, by the Congregation Sheeres Israel for valuable services rendered on the past holidays, as the Shachrith[108] reader. We learn that the presentation took place at the house of Mr. M. Harris, the Vice-President and that all had a happy warm feeling and rejoiced over the event.

Through the kindness of Max Mierson, Esq., a noted young Jewish attorney of this city, we were presented with a copy of "Commercial Law and Mercantile Forms," of which he is the author; he places in it before the public, a plain correct and concise summary of the general rules and abstract principles of mercantile law, also gives various forms, and instructions how to be your own lawyer, we find the book very useful and almost indispensable to businessmen; as it furnished them sufficient knowledge how to avoid lawsuits and unnecessary legal complications. We learn that the same is now used in nearly every mercantile college and we doubt not but what the gentleman will easily dispose of the book and thereby be compensated for his labor.

---

[108]Usually *Shaharith* or *Shacharith*, it is pronounced sach-reeth with a gutteral - ch. It means "morning." On every day throughout the year there are three services: evening, morning, and afternoon. The central elements of the morning service are the Shema, the Eighteen Benedictions, and the added "Blessings of the Morning."

This being our last week in St. Louis, we take occasion to thank all our friends, particularly Dr. Messing and his most charming family, for courtesies extended to us during our stay in the city.

A full description of all institutions of this city will be furnished to our readers, by our able contributor here; and with this statement we trust to be relieved of our promise given heretofore. However, we will not fail to mention that Dr. Messing, Rabbi of the United Hebrew Congregation, has been lately re-elected for two years, by a unanimous vote of all members, which indeed is flattering to the Doctor, as his time does not expire until March next. Members of the congregation understand how to appreciate the services of such a true man as Dr. Messing.

Now once more for the Sunny South, we bid adieu to all our friends.

C. W.

Letter Number Twenty-four

Charles Wessolowsky to Rabbi Edward B. M. Browne

Jackson, Mississippi
13 October 1879

● ● ●

[*On the way back from St. Louis, Wessolowsky stops at Jackson, Mississippi where he describes the Jewish community of about twelve families; while he applauds the presence of a temple, he bemoans the lack of attendance at services.*]

● ● ●

Wednesday evening we departed from St. Louis, and in the cars of the "Cairo Short Line," the connecting line of the Chicago, New Orleans and Jackson R. R., which are fitted up elegantly, and in every way arranged and calculated for the comfort of the traveling public, with polite and attentive conductors, we found ourselves once more en route for the Sunny South. Nothing of special interest demanding our attention having transpired while on the cars, we rocked along in haste and speed, for which the above road is famous, until we reached Jackson, our stopping place.

Our first visit was to meet our genial and intelligent friend Mr. Isidore Strauss, who was glad to see us, and we were soon introduced by him to all our co-religionists, whom we found to be clever, enterprising and possessed of the Southern hospitality.

Jackson, the Capital of Mississippi, numbers about seven thousand inhabitants, among whom we find about twelve Jewish families and in all perhaps seventy-five Jewish souls.

Our brothers here are all engaged in mercantile pursuits and the majority of them seem to do well and prosper. While we deplore the fact that there is no Sabbath School existing here, wherein the youth may receive religious instruction, and to imbue their minds with principles and tenets of our religion, yet Judaism is not altogether neglected here, and our co-religionists in Jackson are willing and ready to bestow their might upon everything that is for the elevation and glory of Judaism. We visited the temple Friday evening, but to our great regret found the attendance to be so slim, that no services were held, and we again left with the question upon our lips, why is it that our brothers will build elegant and grand temples and not even bestow one single hour of their week's time to hold communion with their Creator? Why is it that Jews in their zeal and enthusiasm for our religion, will exhibit their liberality with dollars and cents, and not with their personal attention, to the wants and the requirements of the same? But this question repeatedly asked has become a problem, which will remain unanswered until the dawn of that day, when our Jews will ascertain and to their shame, find that כי לא על הלחם לבדו יחיה האדם [109] the *golden calf* alone does not constitute the happiness of man, and that religion in its pure and untarnished state, with its teaching of morality and truthfulness, is also essential and requisite for the unalloyed pleasure and felicity of this world.

The past holidays have been strictly observed by our brothers in Jackson, Messrs. Henry Strauss and Lazarus Kahn reading the prayers and Mr. Isidor Strauss delivering several lectures. We were told that these gentlemen officiated in a very efficient manner, and certainly deserve the credit and thanks of our co-religionists in Jackson. Will these gentlemen also see to the establishment of a Sabbath School? Give it a trial, and no doubt that with your influence and determination you must succeed, and thereby, receive the thanks of many mothers in Israel, who, through this religious and moral training of their offspring will soon realize their fondest hopes, entertained, when the babe was nestled in their hearts. It is certainly deserving a fair trial and you gentlemen in your capacity ought to be champions and advocates of the same.

The city of Jackson, although a small place, yet with its lofty and stately capitol, street cars, and many other imposing and grand structures, has a "city-like" appearance, and may be styled a handsome price.

On Saturday, it exhibited life and the staff of life, "traffic and trade," and at nights greenbacks were so plentiful that the Hon. Zelon Chase, the champion of the Greenback Party all the way down from Maine, in a speech counted them by the millions. The gentleman seems to *chase* the Democratic and Republican Party, in his hot pursuit forgets that in the main Greenback arguments and

---

[109]Translated, this passage means, "Man does not live by bread alone."

principles are out of date; and that it is useless to introduce *Mississippi* to what the gentleman cannot make effective in his own home, Maine. Mr. Chase spoke for about two hours, and when he finished we could not find the answer to the question "who has got my hay," and thus the *hog* and *hay* will remain upon their old principles and the Greenback Party with their new principles at the next "hog-killing time" will be slaughtered, salted, pickled, and barrelled with the label on the head "never to be opened as in this meat we find the 'Trichinae'."

By the kindness of Mr. Isidore Strauss we enjoyed a ride through the city, and we hereby extend our thanks to his most charming family for courtesies bestowed upon us while in Jackson.

Saturday night we left and Sunday morning found ourselves once more in the presence of our friends, in the Crescent City [New Orleans]; enjoying the greetings and welcomes of our associates and well-wishers.

C. W.

• Part Three •

The Letters and Southern Jewish History

When I came South as a brash New York-born-and-bred Jew in his early twenties to continue my studies in history at the University of North Carolina, I did so with some hesitation and a good deal of trepidation. My uncertainty did not stem from any question about the quality of the university I was about to enter. For a "true-blue Tar Heel," as I now pride myself to be, that would be an admission bordering on heresy. Rather, I suppose I had been conditioned, on the one hand by the provincial self-preoccupation that seems too often to go along with being reared in "*The* City" and by an inbred disbelief that any Jews lived, could live, or wanted to live outside the northern metropolises. On the other hand, I would have had no quarrel with most historians and scholars of Southern history like Wilbur Cash who characterized the Jew with the stereotyped statement that he was "everywhere the eternal alien; and in the South . . . he was especially so."[1] Indeed, my reluctance to step across the Mason-Dixon line was rooted in what I later discovered was an unfounded conviction that everyone "down there," as my friends and relatives disdainfully described the region, wore soiled bed sheets and went around lynching "niggers" and beating up "kikes." And yet, in the course of eighteen years of living in the South, after finding myself ordering ice tea with my lunch during a visit to New York in the dead of winter, and after having experienced nothing like the anti-Semitism I had expected, I began to wonder whether my experience was the exception or whether the

---

[1]Wilbur Cash, *The Mind of the South* (New York: Alfred Knopf, 1975), p. 334.

key events upon which Cash rested his assessment were isolated. As I increasingly pondered this question, another statement I had read begun to gnaw at me. "The Jews were not aliens in a Promised land," wrote Eli Evans, a North Carolina-born Jew, in his widely acclaimed *The Provincials*, "but blood-and-bones part of the South itself—Jewish Southerners."[2]

I approached this contradiction between expectation and experience, as well as that of the two representative opposing viewpoints, from two angles. The first was from the personal position of a Northern-born Jew now living in the South who could not decide whether his two Georgia-born sons were Jews living in the South or Southerners who happened to be Jewish. As one of the very few historians whose field of study is Southern Jewish history, my second approach was naturally an academic one. Consequently, I developed an insatiable appetite for any and all literature dealing with the Southern Jewish experience in my quest to resolve this issue. Did all these articles and books contain some self-evident truth that would allow Cash or Evans to vanquish the other in this debate? To my utter dismay and surprise, the answer to that question was an assured, No! On the contrary, the only result of reading what literature did exist was to add another paradox, or, rather, another and compounding contradiction.

Eli Evans was right. Jews had been living in the region ever since there had been a South. Indeed, most people in both the North and South, if I may be permitted to use those oversimplified socio-geographical categories, would be surprised to learn that in 1800 Charleston had the largest Jewish community in America; that the Jewish congregations in Richmond, Charleston, and Savannah constituted half of the colonial Jewish congregations; and that the South, not the North, was the center of American Jewish life until the Civil War. It would come as an equal shock to these people to learn that it was in the Southern states that the Jews first experienced the freedoms for which the United States would become a bastion. Virginia, South Carolina, and Georgia were the first states to grant Jews political equality. The first Jewish vote in America was cast in South Carolina. The first Jewish United States

---

[2]Eli Evans, *The Provincials* (New York: Atheneum, 1974), p. ix.

Senator was David Yulee (1810-1886), of Florida, who soon was joined by Judah P. Benjamin (1811-1884) of Louisiana. The first Jew to serve as a state governor was probably David Emmanuel (1744-1810), of Georgia.

Utilizing their freedoms, these Jews became a part of Southern society, made their presence felt, and wove their contributions through the Southern fabric. The honor rolls of prominent personages are filled with the names and achievements of Jewish residents. During the American Revolution the list of Southern patriots includes Captain Jacob de la Motta, Captain Jacob de Leon, and Francis Salvador, all from South Carolina; and Colonel Mordecai Sheftall, Sheftall Sheftall, Abraham Simons, and the Minis family, all of Georgia. During the first half of the nineteenth century, Jews continued to serve the region in a way inversely proportional to their small number with, for example, such exploits as David Yulee's vigorous effort to gain Florida's admittance into the Union. (Yulee's ardor in this endeavor was matched only by his equally vigorous effort to get Florida to join the Confederacy.)

During the Civil War, the Jews of the South embraced the South's cause as promptly and enthusiastically as did other Southerners. Almost every Southern regiment had its contingent of Jews who served not only in the ranks, but as sergeants and officers as well. Among the Confederate leadership stood Judah P. Benjamin, known as the "brains of the Confederacy," who served as attorney general, secretary of war and secretary of state. There was David de Leon, the Confederacy's first surgeon-general; Lionel Levy, judge advocate of the military court; and A. C. Myers, quartermaster general.

After the Civil War, when the South lay in ruins, the yet-to-be-recorded Jewish role in raising the South up from her ashes was crucial. The story of Rich's in Atlanta, Neiman-Marcus in Dallas, Sanger's in Galveston, Thalheimer's in Richmond, Maas Brothers in Tampa, and Godchaux in New Orleans is not just a tale of the building of isolated department store empires, but of the Jewish contribution to the economic recovery of the South. As at other times and in other instances, these few names are merely the "tip of the iceberg." Below the surface, as Wessolowsky's letters indicate, are the countless unnamed peddlers and shopkeepers, pioneers of new industries, inventors, doctors, lawyers, newspaper editors, postmasters and postmistresses, speakers of state houses, state representatives and state senators, aldermen and city councilmen, state and city treasurers, judges, sheriffs, police chiefs, court clerks, masonic lodge officers rising as high as state Grand Masters, and so on.

Yet, compared to the tremendous literature available that deals with the Jewish experience in America as a whole, the number of creditable works which deal specifically with the Southern Jewish experience is almost negligible. What little has been written on the subject falls into several categories. The first category is what might be called short (five to fifteen pages) "classical chronicles," which if taken all together would barely make a book, that list the beginnings of the Jewish presence in various Southern states. These poorly-researched and sketchy articles appeared around the turn of the century in the *Publications of the American Jewish Historical Society*. They were written under the auspices of the newly formed American Jewish Historical Society[3] of New York with the intent of combating a growing nativism that emphasized the non-American nature of Jews by both documenting the respectability of American Jewry and demonstrating the Jewish right to American citizenship by reason of longevity.[4] Once having laid claim to the enjoyment of

---

[3]The interest in the American Jewish experience was formally proclaimed with the founding of the American Jewish Historical Society on 7 June 1892, in New York City. The need to collect and preserve the records of the native Jewish population, albeit the colonial South and contemporary Northeast, was a serious concern of Abram Isaacs, Bernard Felsenthal, Leo Levi, and Cyrus Adler. At the Society's first meeting, Oscar Strauss, its first president, proclaimed, "Every nation, race, and creed, which contributed toward the building of this great continent and country, should from motives of patriotism gather up its records and chronicles, so that our historians may be able to examine and describe the forces of our national and political existence." For over fifty years the Society was housed in the buildings of the Jewish Theological Seminary of America in New York City. In 1968, it moved into its own building on the campus of Brandeis University at Waltham, Mass. The Society has published 58 volumes of its *Publications* which became a quarterly in volume 38, and in volume 51 was entitled *American Jewish Historical Quarterly*, and became *American Jewish History* in 1978. It also publishes selected monographs, arranges exhibitions, holds conferences, and has become one of the largest depositories of Jewish records and memorabilia in the country.

[4]Jacob Ezekiel, "The Jews of Richmond," *Publication of the American Jewish*

the American birthright, these well-intentioned "amateurs" continued to use their "historical" writings as a means of promoting self-respect, primarily among the overwhelming numbers of Jews living in the Northeast; and as they turned their attention to chronicling the deeds of these Jews, they directed the attentions of future scholars for decades to come. This legacy of increasing neglect of the Southern Jewish experience fostered another category of writings dealing with Jews in the South different from the first only in the size of the work. The writers, with rare exception, were ill-trained laymen whose enthusiasm could not overcome poor scholarship. These books were community or congregational histories that often were written under local sponsorship and thus too often concentrated on institutional development and the activities of the community's elite. Too often such works were little more than random collections of newspaper clippings, unimpressive biographical sketches, genealogical charts, quotes taken from congregational records, lists of officers and businessmen and professionals, photographs, and anecdotes.[5] The

Historical Society 4 (1896): 21-27; H. Hollander, "The Civil Status of the Jews in Maryland, 1634-1776," *PAJHS* 2 (1894): 33-44; Leon Huehner, "The Jews of Georgia in Colonial Times," *PAJHS* 10 (1902): 65-92; "The Jews of Virginia from the Earliest Times to the Close of the Eighteenth Century," *PAJHS* 20 (1911): 85-105; "The Jews of North Carolina prior to 1800," *PAJHS* 29 (1925), 137-148; Lewis Dembitz, "Jewish Beginnings in Kentucky," *PAJHS* 2 (1893): 99-101; Alfred G. Moses, "A History of the Jews of Mobile," *PAJHS* 12 (1904): 113-25; "The History of the Jews of Montgomery," *PAJHS* 13 (1905): 83-88; Abram Simon, "Notes of Jewish Interest in the District of Columbia," *PAJHS* 26 (1918): 211-18.

[5]Barnett Elzas, *The Jews of South Carolina: From the Earliest Times to the Present Day* (New York: Lippincott, 1905); Herbert T. Ezekiel and Gaston Lichtenstein, *The History of the Jews of Richmond, from 1769 to 1917* (Richmond: Herbert T. Ezekiel, 1917); Milton Altfield, *The Jew's Struggle for Religious and Civil Liberty in Maryland* (Baltimore: n.p. 1924); Julian Feibelman, *A Social and Economic Study of the New Orleans Jewish Community* (Philadelphia: Jewish Publication Society of America, 1941); Isidor Blum, *The Jews of Baltimore* (Baltimore: Historical Review Publishing Co., 1910); Miriam K. Freund, *Jewish Merchants in Colonial American* (New York: Behrman's Jewish Book House, 1939); Charles Reznkoff and Uriah Engelman, *The Jews of Charleston: A History of an American Jewish Community* (Philadelphia: Jewish Publication Society of America, 1950); Jacob Marcus, *Memoirs of American Jews, 1775-1865,* 3 vols. (Philadelphia: Jewish Publication Society of America, 1955-1956); *Early American Jewry,* 2 vols. (Philadelphia: Jewish Publication Society of America, 1951-1953).

purpose of these efforts (no matter that the books printed in limited editions were not widely read) was no different from that of the preceding writings, namely, to gain respectability among the Southern Gentile majority and a self-respect that would offset being ignored by the majority of their co-religionists in other regions. "That's why," one such author who prefers to remain anonymous told me, "we should only write about the good things and the important people whom we can be proud about." Reacting to this violation of my academic sensibilities, I retorted with a question, "Is it right to replace one prejudiced stereotype with another?" And then calling upon an "original" thought, I continued, "Do two wrongs make a right?" With a shrug of the shoulders and a casual nod of the head, this person replied, "Better we should be pictured with halos and wings than with horns and pitchforks."

It is no wonder, then, that there does not exist *one* objective, keen, mind-stirring study of any Jewish community in the South that deals with the patterns of life lived by the less distinguished Jews, a study that goes beyond the surface events to search out what the Jews of the South felt, what they hoped, and what they feared. Those less distinguished, "ordinary" Jews have enjoyed very little, if any, historical notice.

The last category, into which this volume falls, is a mixture of those works that continue the traditions laid down by the writings in the other categories and those few works that reflect the coming of age for Southern Jewish historiography with attempts to delve into the inner mechanics of Jewish communities, the inner thoughts of the Jews themselves, the relationships with white and black Gentiles, and the oftentimes less-than-glowing activities and attitudes of members of the Jewish communities. Unfortunately, the quality work in this field is restricted to short, specialized articles. The monographs that deal with the Jewish experience in the South give the impression of imbalanced and incomplete dissertations that were rushed into print to take advantage of the heightened awareness of Jews living in the South and a desire to know more about them.[6]

---

[6]Steven Hertzberg, *Strangers Within the Gate City, The Jews of Atlanta, 1845-1915* (Philadelphia: Jewish Publication Society of America, 1978); Leonard Dinnerstein, *The Leo Frank Case* (New York: Columbia University Press, 1968);

There are several reasons that might explain why very little material dealing with the Jews in the South exists beyond chronicles and image-making "vainity" publications. For one thing, the sheer numbers of Jews living in Northern metropolises is so overwhelming that the region has overshadowed the rest of the United States. People always go where the action is. As the Southern-born or Southern-raised Jewish families moved north just before and after the Civil War to make their mark in American society, the overriding tendency was to follow them and focus attention on them as the incarnation of Jewish respectability, achievement and contribution to the American experiment.[7] In

Mark Elovitz, *A Century of Jewish Life in Dixie: The Birmingham Experience* (University, Ala.: University of Alabama Press, 1974); Fedora Frank, *Five Families and Eight Young Men: Nashville and Her Jewry, 1850-1861* (Nashville: Fedora Frank, 1962); *Beginning on Market Street: Nashville and Her Jewry, 1861-1901.* (Nashville: Fedora Frank, 1975); Louis Ginsberg, *History of the Jews of Petersburg, 1789-1950* (Petersburg: n.p., 1954); Bertram Korn, *The Jews of Mobile, Alabama, 1763-1841* (Cincinnati: American Jewish Archives, 1970); Morris Speizman, *The Jews of Charlotte* (Charlotte: McNally and Loften, 1978); Sol Beton, *Sephardim and a History of Congregation Or VeShalom* (Atlanta: Congregation Or VeShalom, 1981); Kenneth Stein, A *History of the Ahavath Achim Congregation, 1887-1977* (Atlanta: Standard Press, 1978) ; Janice O. Rothschild, *As But a Day: The First Hundred Years, 1867-1967* (Atlanta: The Hebrew Benevolent Congregation, 1967); Myron Berman, *Richmond's Jewry, 1769-1976* (Charlottesville: University of Virginia Press, 1979); Bertram Korn, *Early Jews of New Orleans* (Waltham, Mass.: American Jewish Historical Society, 1969); Leo Shpall, *The Jews in Louisiana* (New Orleans: n.p., 1936); Isaac Fein, *The Making of an American Jewish Community: The History of Baltimore Jewry from 1773 to 1920* (Philadelphia: Jewish Publication Society of America, 1971); Leonard Dinnerstein and Mary Palsson, eds., *Jews in the South* (Baton Rouge: Louisiana State University Press, 1973); James Lebeau, "Profile of a Southern Jewish Community," *American Jewish Historical Quarterly* 58 (1968-1969); 429-43; Ben Kaplan, *The Eternal Stranger: A Study of Jewish Life in the Small Community.* (New York: Bookman Associates, 1957); Theodore Lowi, "Southern Jews: The Two Communities," *Jewish Journal of Sociology* 6 (1964): 103-17; Arnold Shankman, "Atlanta Jewry, 1900-1930," *American Jewish Archives* 25 (1973): 131-55; Louis Schmier, "Helloo! Peddlerman! Helloo!," in Jerrell Shofner and Linda Ellsworth, eds., *Ethnic Minorities in Gulf Coast Society* (Pensacola: Gulf Coast Historical and Humanities Conference, 1979); Nathan Kaganoff and Melvin I Urofsky, eds., *Turn To the South* (Charlottesville: University of Virginia Press, 1979).

[7]Stephen Birmingham, *Our Crowd* (New York: Harper & Row, 1967).

simple terms, this was the pattern of investigation of those who founded the American Jewish Historical Society: scan the Southern roots during the colonial, revolutionary and ante-bellum periods; concentrate on the second half of the nineteenth century when these people made their marks; and continue to make a case for the millions of immigrants who were pouring into the country in the twentieth century. Consequently, not only did people become accustomed to looking to the Northeast as the perennial center of Jewish life in America, but, whenever the story of the American Jew has been studied in the past, the emphasis had always been on the urban Northeast as if the sole drama of Jewish America had been played there. The Jews living in the South were generally ignored and overlooked; and any description that might include the Jews living in the South was treated as a prologue of the great things to come in the North. Of those Jews who were silly enough to remain in the South or migrate to the South, the attitude was that they should be treated as "country cousins," peripheral to the main story, a curious sideshow, but of no consequence when compared to the events in the main Northeast arena.

This tendency was reinforced by the available research material needed to study American Jewry. Because this collection was begun by and continued under the legacy of the early founders of the American Jewish Historical Society, apologists of the American Jewish experience, already influenced by their desire to sanitize the Jewish presence in America and to project a patriotic image of the Jew, were drawn like bees to honey by the activities of admittedly American Jewish leaders who lived mostly in the North and by the voluminous cache of records that was building up concerning the entrance of millions of Jewish immigrants and their collected actions in the Northern cities. Let's face it, the struggles of an anonymous Jewish peddler walking the trail in Mississippi were far harder to document and far less attractive than the exploits of the great financier Jacob Schiff. The presence of Jewish newspapers such as *Vorwarts*, the Yiddish theater, the Jewish organizations, the visible activities of Jews in the union movements as well as in all walks of Northern life, and the immigration records and studies of immigrants all forced scholars and amateurs alike to concentrate on the Northern Jewish experience.

The result was two-fold. First, whatever academic attention was given to the Jewish experience was restricted to the North. This was especially true of the students coming out of Northern Universities who merely added to the existing momentum by concentrating their efforts on collecting records and engaging in research in the area to which they were directed by their Northern-oriented and Northern-born mentors. Second, existing institutional and personal records relating to the Southern Jewish experience were neglected. The lack of such groups of records seems, then, to lend further support to the existing attitudes. It was like saying: "If the Jews in the South were so important, why didn't they preserve their records? Since they did not, they themselves must have known how unimportant they were to the entire story. We just can't expend our valuable time and limited funds on such tangential matters." What records were preserved were done so by families for personal reasons; by congregations who just happened not to have lost them; and by historical societies, state archives, and university collections which happened to catch inadvertently some Jewish records in the nets they were using to sweep in research material dealing with the South.

It was not until the founding of the American Jewish Archives on the campus of Hebrew Union College at Cincinnati in 1948 under the auspices of Dr. Jacob Marcus that Southern Jewish memorabilia and records were considered truly worthy of preservation for reasons other than those already discussed.[8] Unfortunately, this effort came too late for many records which have been lost to the ravages of time, fire, tornado, flood, rats, cockroaches, mildew, and the garbageman. Without these records it will be even more difficult to write the hitherto unrecognized, unheralded, and unacknowledged stories of the Southern Jewish experience; and it will take a monumental effort to reverse the process of record neglect, damage, and destruction that has been in operation far too long.

---

[8]For a discussion of the program of the American Jewish Archives, see Jacob Marcus and Bertram Korn, "The Program of the American Jewish Archives," *American Jewish Archives* 1 (1948): 2-5. The collection of the Archives is divided into several departments: manuscripts and typescripts, "nearprints," photographs, indices, and publications.

It is equally unfortunate that both the American Jewish Archives and the American Jewish Historical Society, with their broad responsibility of collecting material dealing with the whole of the American Jewish experience, cannot concentrate their efforts to undo decades of neglect. Perhaps now, when the South is emerging as a regional force, may be the time to establish programs at major Southern universities to collect and preserve surviving research material as well as to tell the rich and vital tale of the experience of the Jew in the South; to train others to follow in footpaths being cut by literally less than a handful; and to establish an archival collection comparable to the Southern Collection at the University of North Carolina for the sole purpose of preserving and concentrating the record of the Jew in the South.

Without such a record-preservation program and without the dissemination of this mind-stirring story, another reason for the depreciation of the importance of the Jews living in the South will prevail. That reason is, namely, ignorance which has not allowed the Jewish experience in the South to have equal space with other issues. The preoccupation and fascination with the black-white struggle has not allowed anyone to concentrate on other experiences. "There are Jews down there? I thought only *goys* and *schwartzers* (Gentiles and blacks) live there," exclaimed an acquaintance from Pennsylvania when I told him of the synagogue and congregation in Valdosta, Georgia. So dominating has been the black-white issue, that many people have overlooked the differences that exist within the white population and, therefore, have ignored the story of any white minority—Jew, Catholic, Italian, etc.— in the South. The absence of any recognition, until within the last ten years, that white diversity exists is a reflection of the prevalence of the stereotype of the South as a dull, gray, mono-elemental culture existing apart from the multi-cultural and multi-ethnic America that is called the "melting pot." For anyone who accepts the validity of that stereotype, consciously or subconsciously, seeking out the story of the Jew in the South would be like a blind man trying to find a black cat in a darkened room when the cat is not in the room in the first place.

Finally, the effects of the "loser image" of the South on Southern Jewry cannot be ignored, especially when combined with the condescending attitude of the Northern "city slickers" toward their "country cousins" in the South. Perhaps, in spite of wanting to believe otherwise, Southern Jewry had a sense of inferiority and inadequacy that undermined their confidence and imposed upon them an instinctive shyness that prohibited them, until recently, from standing up and proclaiming aloud: "I will not be ignored! I am important! Look at me!" This inclination to maintain a low profile was reinforced by a sense of isolation from their co-religionists in the North as well as by a sense of being a minority among an overwhelming Gentile majority, and by what may be called a subconscious acceptance of the fact that living "on the rim" proved they did not belong in the center of things.

I offer these reasons for the absence of a viable, creditable, and scholarly Southern Jewish bibliography with Jacob Burkhardt's warning, "Beware of the simplifiers," ringing in my ears, with the realization that more often than not Jews such as those mentioned by Wessolowsky in his letters certainly did not keep a low profile, and with the admission that I am playing at being an amateur psychologist. We may be suspicious of sweeping, general, and catch-all statements such as the one I have just offered, but there is a real, if vague, state of mind such as outlined above that one can sense. It is something one cannot isolate or even put into words. But, as Eli Evans says, it is there.[9] And it has been only in the last ten or fifteen years that one can sense an end to that attitude, or at least a modification of it, as Southern patterns as a whole have been changed by the "discovery" of the South by immigrants from the North such as me, by the recent processes of industrialization and urbanization, and by the immigration of the South northward into Washington and the White House.

Nineteen seventy-six was an auspicious year that has received a number of titles. It is called the Year of the South, the Year of Jimmy Carter, the Bicentennial Year, and—in some circles—the Year of Southern Jewry. These labels are by no means as isolated from each other as one might suppose: as Jimmy Carter won the presidency the South and all those living within it were rediscovered. Part of that reawakening process was a move by Jews

---

[9]Eli Evans, "Southern-Jewish History Alive and Unfolding," in Nathan M. Kaganoff and Melvin I. Urofsky, *Turn to the South* (Charlottesville: University of Virginia Press, 1979), pp. 158-67.

in the South to make their presence known and to win the recognition due them. Reflecting this assertiveness, the American Jewish Historical Society, at the urging of Sol Viener of Richmond and then president of the Society's governing body, sponsored a conference, in the fall of 1976, in Richmond, dealing with the history of Southern Jewry. The response to this conference caught everyone by surprise. It drew participants from as far south as Florida, as far west as Texas, and from all the Northern industrial states. One visible result of that conference was the publication of the papers presented at the conference.[10] Even more important, the success of that conference heralded a slow change in the orientation of the American Jewish Historical Society. In the years that followed, it held its annual meetings for the first time outside the Northeast (in Nashville, Pittsburgh, and San Francisco), and scheduled its 1983 meeting for Savannah to coincide with that Jewish community's 250th anniversary. While the Richmond conference convinced many people that there is Jewish life outside New York, unknown to those at the conference, that meeting provided the catalyst to a milestone event in both American Jewish and Southern Jewish history.

In May of the following year (1977), at the airport in Raleigh-Durham, N.C., four men met, just as those enthusiastic amateurs met in New York in 1892 to found the American Jewish Historical Society, and for a similar purpose. Those four men had attended the Richmond conference and had witnessed the enthusiasm of the conferees and had taken notice of the work that had to be done in promoting the story of the Jewish experience in the South. Out from that modest meeting, the Southern Jewish Historical Society was born with its dedication to insuring that the Richmond conference was not an isolated shot-in-the-dark, and that the commitment to support future research, publications, conferences, and exhibits dealing with the Southern Jewish experience would continue.[11]

---

[10]Kaganoff and Urofsky, *Turn to the South.*

[11]The four men who met at the Raleigh-Durham airport were Sol Viener of Richmond, Va., David Goldberg of New Orleans, La., Abram Kanof of Raleigh, N. C., and Louis Schmier of Valdosta, Ga. With the enthusiastic support and direct help of the American Jewish Historical Society the newly born Southern Jewish Historical Society tested its base with a conference on the Southern Jewish experience that was held in Raleigh, N. C., in May 1978. Since then it has had a

Since that eventful day, the Society has slowly grown to a membership of over 350, representing every state in the South and many in the North; it has held four conferences, each in a different Southern city, with two future conferences already booked; it is preparing to publish the papers presented at those conferences; it has supported the publication of manuscripts dealing with Southern Jewry; it was instrumental in the publication of a special issue of the *Atlanta Historical Journal* devoted to the Jews of Georgia;[12] and its future plans include offering stipends for research, campaigning for the establishment of a Southern Jewish record center, and aiding local communities to collect and preserve their records.

This volume containing the letters of Charles Wessolowsky is a product of the recent growth of interest in the Southern Jewish experience, and of the active support provided by the Southern Jewish Historical Society. These letters offer more than a view of the character of a man who was known throughout the South during his lifetime but who has since fallen into historical oblivion. They offer tantalizing glimpses of Jewish communities in the South which no longer exist or whose history of that period has hitherto been lost and forgotten. To be sure, the letters allow only a passing look at these communities; and the look is unfortunately at times as fleeting as the trains and boats and coaches which carried Wessolowsky across the South in the course of his three tours. While we may wish that he had written more letters and longer letters describing in greater detail those communities he had visited, there is enough in the letters we do have to whet the appetite. These letters reveal how little is truly known of Southern Jews of that particular time and how much work needs to be done to recover what is left of their story.

---

cycle of annual fall conferences: Savannah in 1978; Charleston in 1979; Jacksonville in 1980. It is scheduled for Mobile in 1981; New Orleans in 1982; and Atlanta in 1983. While it is too young and its funds are too limited to be based in any permanent location and to possess an archives of its own, it works closely with the American Jewish Archives and the American Jewish Historical Society to collect and preserve records, as well as to disseminate the surfacing story of the Jew in the South. Its present address is Southern Jewish Historical Society; VSC Box 179; Valdosta, Ga. 31698.

[12]*Atlanta Historical Journal*, 23, No. 3 (Fall 1979).

Because most of the previous writings dealing with the Jews in the South were poorly researched and were written as the result of a hobby-like interest in history, the ability and desire to search out hidden and distant records were absent. Where newspapers did not exist and where congregations never existed, the Jewish experience remains hidden and inadequately understood. The view of the Jews in those towns described by Wessolowsky, then, offers an opportunity to retrieve a few of the lost threads with which the fabric of Southern Jewish life was woven. We can get an overview of how these Jews dealt with the social, political, economic, and religious issues confronting them as minorities living among an alien Gentile majority. We can briefly perceive the various engagements in the struggle "to belong," to modify Old World traditions to the New World in which they now lived, to decide the means by which and the extent to which they would change, and to decide how visibly and actively Jewish they would remain. At the same time, each letter shows how different were the answers to the questions the Jews asked of themselves, how individual were the solutions they offered to their problems of adjustment, how diverse was the modification of the traditional liturgy, how far they ventured into Gentile social and political circles, and how much they were willing to pay with their Jewish consciousness and commitment for a place within the society in which they lived.

Equally important, these letters, with their personal and often intimate illuminations, begin to offer the hitherto absent criteria by which to judge whether the Jewish experience in the South is unique. In fact, those generalizations that have been applied to the Jews in the South in attempts to analyze their experience have been derived largely from studies of major population centers in the Northeast with a few studies of smaller communities sprinkled in. The consequences have been too often that conclusions drawn from those studies have been applied to Jews living throughout the country without any indication that such a widespread application of such conclusions is valid. In the absence of studies on the local level, and in the absence of insights into the personal life of a Jewish community, however brief that look may be, it is impossible, on the one hand, to validate any generalizations regarding institutional life, economic achievement, social structure, ethnic and religious identity, internal unity or fracture, or communal relations with the

Gentile majority and other minorities. On the other hand, without such insights into the inner thinking of the Southern Jews at both the individual and community level, it would be impossible to form new and modifying judgment, and the old myths and stereotypes would prevail.

Certainly, two myths must be questioned, since they are undermined by Wessolowsky's observations. The first is what Cash expresses as follows: "the Jew, with his universal refusal to be assimilated. . .had always stood out with great vividness."[13] The second is that the South is a violent and savage place in which all minorities fear for their lives. Would that life were that simple! If we tear through the opaque curtains of the stereotype that the South is the most anti-Semitic region in the country, the reading of Wessolowsky's letter might help us to start getting down to the most important subtleties. While it is true that the sensational lynching of Leo Frank of Atlanta in 1915 hung like an albatross around the image of the South and hovered like a foreboding raven about the heads of Jews, evoking fear and insecurity, most Jews in the South will tell anyone that they do not fear for their safety. Attempts to sweep aside the disparity between the studies which conclude that the South is the most anti-Semitic region in the country and those that show that more acts of violence and threats are directed against Jews living in the north, and between the perception of how Southern Jews "should" feel and how they themselves perceive the South, point to a number of over-simplifications. First, since there are more Jews in the North, incidents against them *should* be higher in number, but, by percentage, they are greater in the South. Second, the absence of overt incidents do not indicate the depth of prejudice that would surface if the social stability of the Gentile society was ever seemingly threatened. Third, the presence of blacks acts as a lightning rod to attract antagonistic attitudes which otherwise might be directed against the Jews. That is to say, either the Jews are considered white first and live as part of the white majority, or the Gentiles are so busy hating blacks that they have little time for the Jews, or, having vented their spleen on the blacks, they were satisfied.[14]

---

[13]Cash, *Mind of the South*, p. 334.

[14]Charles Y. Glock and Rodney Stark, *Christian Beliefs and Anti-Semitism*

Indeed, one woman said to me during an interview, "My grandmother always used to say about them hating the blacks, 'Better it should be that way. Too long it was us. Now it is their turn'."[15] On the other side, a ninety-two year old woman told me, "Hate the Jews? Never! They were people of the Book! Now those papists, they were something else. Mama used to warn me that if'n I was ever caught even so much as walking on the same side of the street as a Catholic my soul would sure enough go to hell."[16] Yet a third person said, in a different vein, "Loved the Jews, yes sir, loved the Jews!" "Why?," I asked him, thinking I would get an answer related to their biblical heritage. But his answer caught me by surprise. He leaned over with one hand on his rocking chair arm and, pointing his finger at my nose, squinted his eyes and forcefully said, "Because my daddy didn't want us to be actin' like those damn papists!"[17]

All of this suggests that life in the South is more complicated, variable, ambivalent and inconsistent once we get away from the "tobacco road" and "big daddy" syndromes, and that certain idiosyncrasies must be taken into account. A major syndrome, strongly hinted at in Wessolowsky's letters, is that if fear works vocally or silently to modify attitudes and actions—the "what will the *goyim* think" syndrome—such alterations are also the product of the outstretched hand of acceptance or access to position. Always keeping in mind what a theologian once suggested to me, that anti-Semitism is deeply rooted in the theological psyche of the Christian, various factors have to be taken into consideration as possibly helping to neutralize anti-Semitic beliefs and actions. How did the economic services provided by the Jewish peddlers and merchants undermine anti-Semitism? To what extent did the involvement of Jews in the Confederacy affect Gentile attitudes? How much did

(New York: Harper & Row, 1966); Gertrude Selznick and Stephen Steinberg, *The Tenacity of Prejudice: Anti-Semitism in Contemporary America* (New York: Harper & Row, 1969); Oscar Cohen, "Public Opinion and Anti-Jewish Prejudice in the South," a paper delivered to the National Executive Committee Meeting of the Anti-Defamation League of B'nai B'rith, 25 September 1969, New Orleans, La.

[15]Interview with Claire Freedman, Savannah, Ga., 16 December 1975.

[16]Interview with Mrs. Arthur Strom, Valdosta, Ga., 12 December 1975.

[17]Interview with Ira Treadaway, Quitman, Ga., 30 January 1978.

admiration for the Jewish work ethic influence the actual treatment of Jews? Being white and having closer contact with the Gentiles, how did personal relationships overcome impersonal stereotypes of Jews? Did "Southern hospitality" have an ameliorating consequence? What was the extent and consequence of the presence of a religious "pro-Semitism"? I can recall innumerable statements made by both Jew and Gentile during interviews I conducted for another project that seem to support the credence of asking these questions. And while I am reminded by the warning of an old Jewish saying, "a 'for instance' is not proof," there is sufficient indication that such statements may reflect attitudes that are not necessarily the exception.

Wessolowsky's letters provide sufficient evidence to indicate that it is time to put to rest these prejudicial simplicities that have been applied to both Jews and Gentiles living in the South. We should use his letters, however, not to create an acceptable provincialism of Southern Jews and Southern Gentiles. To fall into that trap would be just as much a stumbling block to reality as was the existence of a New York provincialism. While a good measure of provincialism is necessary for the attainment of a regional and local identity, ultimately its use is for the purpose of seeing how the part fits into the whole. In other words, Wessolowsky's letters might help us start assisting Eli Evans and other Southern Jews, as well as Southern Gentiles, in solving the problem Evans stated in his *The Provincials*: "I was certain that Southern Jews were molded by the ethos they grew up in, and I wanted to reach for the nuances of the Southerner's attitudes toward the Jews . . . and the gap between the life I led and the South they wrote about always bothered me. . . . We were Jews; we were Southerners. I was never sure what either meant, nor how they came together."[18] I cannot answer the question that lurks in Eli Evan's mind. Unfortunately, no one else can as yet fulfill that task either. Perhaps, however, Wessolowsky's letters can give us insights into that sought-after solution.

---

[18]Evan, *The Provincials*, p. xi.

Appendix 1

Active lodges of the B'nai B'rith in the Southern states during 1878-1879 as listed in the *Report of the Fourth Meeting of District No. 5 Grand Lodge* and in the *Secretary's Report District No. 7 Grand Lodge, 1879*

Town or City	Lodge Name & Number	Town or City	Lodge Name & Number
District No. 5 Grand Lodge			
Albany, GA	Mica 147	Selma, AL	Zadok 155
Americus, GA	Raphael 145	Uniontown, AL	Concordia 152
Atlanta, GA	Gate City 144	Camden, AR	Elah 282
Augusta, GA	Obadiah 119	Fort Smith, AR	Fort Smith 306
Bainbridge, GA	Libnah 234	Helena, AR	Esther 159
Brunswick, GA	Misdol 318	Hot Springs, AR*	Hot Springs 278
Columbus, GA	Columbus 77	Little Rock, AR	Little Rock 158
Macon, GA	Malachi 146	Pine Bluff, AR	Phoenix 279
Savannah, GA	St. Joseph 76	Pine Bluff, AR	Pine Bluff 307
Savannah, GA	Savannah 217	Jacksonville, FL	Jacksonville 287
Thomasville, GA	Georgia 207	Pensacola, FL	Alpha 219
Charlotte, NC	Charlotte 280	Alexandria, LA	Rebecca 240
Tarboro, NC	Zanoah 235	Bastrop, LA	Hanna 276
Wilmington, NC	North State 222	Baton Rouge, LA	Abraham Geiger 232
Charleston, NC	Dan 93	Bayou Sara, LA	Bayou Sara 162
Alexandria, VA	Mount Vernon 259	Clinton, LA	Feliciana 239
Charlottesville, VA	Montecello 214	Farmersville, LA	Farmersville 277
Harrisburg, VA	Elah 204	Monroe, LA	Adasa 208
Norfolk, VA	Maon 172	Natchitoches, LA	Othniel 274
Peterburg, VA	Virginia 225	New Iberia, LA	Attakapas 284
Richmond, VA	Benjamin 69	New Orleans, LA	B'nai Israel 188
Richmond, VA	Paradise 223	New Orleans, LA	Crescent City 182
Richmond, VA	Rimmon 68	New Orleans, LA	Gulf 221
District No. 7 Grand Lodge		New Orleans, LA	Home 243
Demopolis, AL	Marengo 283	New Orleans, LA	Orleans 220
Eufaula, AL	Jephthah 142	Opelousas, LA	Zered 245
Huntsville, AL	Esora 236	St. Joseph	Zidkijah 297
Mobile, AL	Beth Zur 84	Shreveport, LA	Louisiana 107
Montgomery, AL	Alabama 209	Canton, MS	Judith 106
Montgomery, AL	Emmanual 103	Columbus, MS	Joachim 181

Town or City	Lodge Name & Number	Town or City	Lodge Name & Number
Durant, MS	N. D. Menken 317	Austin, TX	Hill City 241
Greenville, MS	Amity 267	Brenham, TX	Akiba Eger 249
Greenville, MS	Deborah 161	Corsicana, TX	Corsicana 275
Meridian, MS	Asaph 286	Dallas, TX	Dallas 197
Natchez, MS	Ezra 134	Fort Worth, TX*	Fort Worth 269
Port Gibson, MS	Raphidim 230	Galveston, TX	Zacharia Fraenkel 242
Summit, MS	Ruth 262	Halletsville, TX	Naomi 313
Vicksburg, MS	Enrogel 233	Houston, TX	Lone Star 210
Vicksburg, MS	Vicksburg 98	Jefferson, TX	Alamo 290
Jackson, MS	Manasseh 202	Jewett, TX	Jewett 305
Brownsville, TN	West Tennessee 316	Marshall, TX	Reuben 257
Chattanooga, TN	Lookout Mountain 194	Rockdale, TX	Rockdale 229
Memphis, TN	Euphrates 35	San Antonio, TX	Edar 211
Memphis, TN	Hiddekel 100	Sherman, TX	Nahum 300
Memphis, TN	Simon Tuska 192	Victoria, TX	Victoria 212
Nashville, TN	Maimonides 46	Waco, TX	Eureka 198

*Disbanded or suspended in late 1879

Appendix 2

Active lodges of the Independent Order of the Free Sons of Israel in the Southern states during 1878-1883 as listed in: *Proceedings of the General Convention of the United States Grand Lodge of the Independent Order Free Sons of Israel held in the City of Rochester, February 23d, 24th, 25th, 26th, & 27th* (New York: Independent Order Free Sons of Israel, 1879), p. 93-96; *Convention of the Independent Order Free Sons of Israel, Cincinnati, February 1884* (New York: Independent Order Free Sons of Israel, 1884), pp. 268-70.

State	Town or City	Lodge Name & Number	Date Organized
Ark.	Pine Bluff	Eureka 36	21 October 1877
Ga.*	Atlanta	Atlanta 85	5 December 1877
La.**	New Orleans	Louisiana 88	1 January 1879
Miss.	Greenville	James A. Garfield 91	1 January 1882
	Port Gibson	Mississippi 75	9 September 1883
	Vicksburg	Joseph Simmons 84	7 October 1877
Mo.***	St. Joseph	Missouri 99	2 September 1879
	St. Louis	George Washington 82	14 January 1877
	St. Louis	Judah Touro 4	15 April 1873
	St. Louis	Progress 53	6 September 1872
Tenn.	Nashville	Gal Ed 81	26 March 1876
Texas	Dallas	Lone Star 97	3 August 1879
Va.****	Richmond	Friendship 47	28 July 1872

*Macon City Lodge 102 organized 10 February 1884 in Macon, Georgia.

**While Wessolowsky mentions the existence of a lodge in Shreveport in letter No. 19, it apparently never affiliated with the Grand Lodge on an official basis.

***Pride of the West Lodge 96 organized 14 December 1884 in St. Louis, Missouri.

****Edmund Lasker Lodge 101 organized 10 February 1884 in Norfolk, Virginia.

Index